Camping and Hiking

This is a new book – written, designed and illustrated to be a guide for anyone who is going camping or hiking, whether alone, with a few friends, or in a larger party.

From equipment and personal gear to striking camp and packing up at the end, there is something of interest to everyone, however experienced they are. The extra material covers many vital and fascinating aspects of life in the country – maps and compasses, knives and axes, first aid, logs, and nature diaries, weather and safety precautions.

The book is published with the support and approval of the Scout Association, and covers almost all the requirements for the Scout Standard and Advanced Scout Standard.

D0993984

FALCON TRAVIS

Camping and Hiking

*With drawings and diagrams by Leslie Marshall
and cartoons by McLachlan*

 KNIGHT BOOKS

the paperback division of Brockhampton Press

ISBN 340 04143 9

First published 1968 by Brockhampton Press Ltd
This edition published simultaneously by Knight Books,
the paperback division of Brockhampton Press Ltd, Leicester

Second revised impression 1975

Printed and bound in Great Britain by
Richard Clay (The Chaucer Press) Ltd, Bungay, Suffolk

Text copyright © 1968 Falcon Travis
Illustrations copyright © 1968 Brockhampton Press Ltd

Contents

When you get there

Homeward tracks

Introduction

CAMPING and hiking are variously described as hobbies, sports, games, pastimes, and sometimes as recreations and healthy exercise. They can be something of all these, but each is also a craft, and the better a camper or hiker knows his craft, the more he will enjoy his camping or hiking, and the more easily will he be able to combine it with some other interest, such as fishing, photography, bird- or animal-watching, or any of the many other outdoor pursuits that can add to the fun of camping and hiking.

Campers and hikers who are poor at their craft are usually so busy trying to cope that they have little time for anything else.

Before you embark too enthusiastically on the outdoor trail, make sure that it is the life for you. The open-air life is not everybody's idea of fun, though most who make a good start seldom turn back. Give yourself a good trial run before you spend money on equipment. If possible, camp or hike with somebody who really knows the game.

If you do decide that the wide-open spaces are for you, build up your gear gradually, getting the best you can afford. For hiking, start with a rucksack, then walking shoes, and the rest in any order. For camping, start with a rucksack, blankets borrowed from home, and shared cooking gear and tent. Then get a canteen, next a sleeping bag, then a tent (unless you have a long-term sharing arrangement), and the rest in any order.

Scouts have less of a starting problem. They usually begin their camping with their Troop or Patrol, using Group camp gear, and under the guidance of Leaders who are experienced campers, and like most others who get well started along the trail, they go on, ever raising their standard of campcraft.

9

Before you start out

EQUIPMENT

HIKERS, hike-campers, and standing-campers all need equipment of some sort, be it hiker equipping himself with nothing more than a plastic mac stuffed into his jacket pocket, or standing-camper staggering under a knee-buckling load the short distance from the railway station to the camp site. Weighty and bulky equipment matters little to the standing-camper once he gets it to the site, because until the end of his camp it is there to stay. The hike- or cycle-camper normally camps and moves on, walking or cycling miles from one site to the next with all his equipment on his back or in his panniers. Weight is all-important to him. He keeps the total weight of his kit as low as he reasonably can.

If you could see the contents of the rucksacks of a score of campers arriving on a site for a weekend camp, you would be extremely lucky to find two alike. Campers are individualists. Each has his own idea about what is the best shape, colour, and type of tent; the most economical stove; the warmest filling for sleeping bags; the hardest wearing groundsheet; the most serviceable rucksack or cooking pots; and definite opinions on the rest of his gear; and what are essentials and what are not.

Even so, their equipment would be basically the same, because their needs are basically the same – they will all want to eat and drink, and clean their teeth and wash, and sleep warm and sheltered, and so on.

What to Take

Here is a list of personal kit and camp gear suitable for a hike-camp or a lightweight weekend camp, with suggestions for keeping the weight down to a minimum. The total weight, depending on choice of gear, could be between 15 and 20 lb.

How much of this gear the hiker (not camping) should take would depend on the kind of hike planned. You will need the least if you are carrying only sandwiches and a flask (or buying a meal somewhere), and the most if you are doing everything but sleep out. You will choose according to your need.

The new hike-camper tends to take too much at first, but soon gets round to taking only what he needs and no more.

For the small standing-camp, where weight is not a vital factor, alternative and additional items are listed at the end.

Personal Kit

SLEEPING
> *Pyjamas* (or items of spare clothing to save weight and space)
> *Blankets* – 2 (useless if not all-wool)
> *or Sleeping bag* (lighter and less bulky than blankets)
> *Pillow* (light cotton or muslin bag that can be stuffed with spare clothing)

WASHING
> *Towel* (or part of one, or a yard of butter muslin saves weight)
> *Soap* (or half or partly used tablet) in container
> *Toothbrush and paste* (or partly used tube)
> *Comb*
> (*Soap, toothbrush and paste, and comb together in bag*)

EATING

Knife, fork, and spoon (dessert and tea) – together in bag

Mug (half-pint, unbreakable. Not aluminium – gets too hot, burns lips)

Plates – 2 (unless carrying canteen. Unbreakable – enamel or plastic. Deep-sided is less spillable and keeps food warmer longer. Not aluminium – cools too quickly. Not thin plastic – most soften under heat)

EXTRA CLOTHING

Sweater or cardigan (for cool of evening, etc.). Woollen hat also useful

Plimsolls or sandals (without stockings in wet grass)

Waterproof coat, or cape (pouched to cover rucksack, an advantage)

Waterproof headgear (sou'wester, etc.)

SPARE CLOTHING (to include a complete change of clothes)

Shirt

Shorts or longs

Stockings or socks

Underwear

Handkerchiefs

SHARED KIT (with companion or small group)

First-aid outfit; mending kit (needle, cotton, buttons, etc.); *shoe-cleaning materials; small or folding brush; mirror; map and compass*

Camp Gear

SHELTER

Tent (or hike-sheet, with guy-line cord and pegs), *poles and pegs*

Groundsheet

Lighting – small torch – spare bulb and batteries or candle and lantern (flat-folding candle-lantern)

COOKING

Canteen (saucepan(s) and frypan/plate(s). Weight 12 to 16 oz)

Water bucket (wedge-shape stands well, pours well. 1 gallon canvas, weighs 3 oz)

Tin-opener (in clasp knife, or 'baby' can-opener, weighing $\frac{1}{2}$ oz)

Matches (strike-anywhere type. Dipping heads in nail varnish will waterproof)

Stove, paraffin – if not using wood fire (Half-pint size weighs 1 lb 14 oz) *fuel container, windscreen, priming tablets, and prickers*

CLEANING

Dish cloth, or mop, or block sponge with abrasive side

Drying cloth – muslin (light, effective, and quick drying)

Soap, washing (for cloths and clothes)

STORAGE

Muslin (for covering food)

Containers – unbreakable, screw-topped (for jam, fats, butter, etc.)

Bags – cloth or plastic (for tea, sugar, flour, rice, etc.) – string bag (little bulk or weight) useful for shopping, etc.

Milk can or collapsible (polythene, etc.) *container*

SUNDRIES

Trowel, small – for turfing and digging fireplace, latrines, pits, etc. (flattened garden type suitable, or builder's with point ground off)

Wash-bowl – personal use only, not washing-up (canvas – about 4 oz)

Twine – for gadgets, etc.

Paper, latrine

Standing-camp Alternatives and Additions to Hike-camp List

SHELTER

Tents – according to numbers
Store tent, poles, and pegs
Dining shelter, poles, guys, and pegs – if required
Cooking shelter, poles, guys, and pegs – if required
Lighting – hurricane lamps (half-pint size: burning time –
24 hours)

COOKING

Utensils – nesting paint-pot billies, or dixies; frying pans
Kitchen cutlery, wooden spoon, ladle, etc.

CLEANING

Extra according to numbers

STORAGE (FOOD)

Extra according to numbers

SUNDRIES

Spade or entrenching tool instead of trowel
Extra wash bowls as and if required
Axe or bow (bush) saw
Latrine screening, poles, guys and pegs, and lantern
Camp First-aid box
Spare guy cord and pegs

What to Wear

Shorts, shoes, shirt with an open neck, and a zipped windproof jacket, are the popular wear of the experienced walker in the countryside in the summer. Handy in his rucksack will be a sweater for the cooler moments, and a waterproof coat or cape and headgear. There are, of course, variations.

Shorts or longs? Shorts allow freer movement, and are less uncomfortable in wet weather. Long trousers are better in rough and hilly country. Flannel or wool is best. Corduroy is heavy when wet, and slow drying out. Tight trousers restrict movement, cling tighter when wet, and are colder than loose-fitting trousers.

Boots or shoes? Both are suitable for lowland walking, but shoes are lighter, allow the ankles freer movement, and give the feet better ventilation. In rough, hilly country boots are essential. They give the necessary extra support and protection to the ankles.

Walking shoes should be stout and strong, fairly light in weight, and waterproof. Smooth soles will slide on grass (wet or dry) and give you stiff and aching leg muscles, so the soles should be either of the rubber or composition type with a moulded nailing pattern, or of leather with about two dozen light studs per sole and a dozen per heel. The shoes should be

 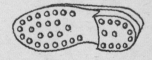

broad enough for the natural spread of the foot when standing, and half a size bigger than normal to allow thick woollen stockings to be worn. Stockings with oversocks are preferable, and it is a good plan to be wearing them when buying walking shoes or boots, and to lace them up and walk the shop in them. They should fit snugly, without any loose movement of the foot, while allowing the toes to move.

Underwear: String or mesh (cellular) materials for underwear are healthier than closely woven ones: air can get to the skin, and perspiration evaporates instead of being retained and making the garment clammy and possibly causing a chill. As air is a poor conductor of heat, partially preventing its passage, a cellular garment keeps the temperature of the body near normal, thus making it seem cooler in summer and warmer in winter. Air between a tent and its fly-sheet is a similar heat barrier.

Outerwear: Shirts and sweaters should be open-necked to allow a free circulation of air to the body.

The anorak, regarded as ungainly and scruffy looking by some, gives better weather protection than the zipped or buttoned windcheater type of jacket. It is longer, is usually hooded, and has roomy pockets. Anorak or jacket, it should be

loose-fitting enough for a sweater or two to be worn underneath. It is also better water-repellent (like a cotton raincoat) than waterproof (like a plastic mac). Waterproofed garments can become quite wet inside with condensed perspiration.

A waterproof garment is necessary for complete wet-weather protection. Lightweight plastic-coated cloth is best. Coat or cape? A coat keeps the arms covered, and has pockets, but it clings closer and so causes more condensation, and it gets abnormal wear from the rucksack and its straps. A cape is more suitable and is cheaper. A good model, with sou'wester to match, now being sold by a reliable supplier, is an ample-length, light-weight, polyurethene (plastic) coated nylon, with arm slits and a gusseted back to cover a rucksack. It buttons down the front, and has shoulder tapes so that the cape can be thrown back over the shoulders.

Packing a Rucksack

A well-packed rucksack looks neat, is evenly balanced and has nothing hanging outside. It has the lighter, bulkier articles at the bottom and the heavier ones at the top, making the pack top-heavy for easier carrying.

For good packing, the rule is: last wanted, first in. To arrive at a site in the rain and have to empty your rucksack out to get at the tent at the bottom would be bad packing. An experienced camper always packs his rucksack in the same general order. It then becomes an easy and quick job, and he knows exactly where he can find anything, even in the dark.

To pack the kit already suggested for a hike-camp or a light-weight weekend camp, the spare clothing, bedding, and other sleeping gear would be at the bottom of the rucksack; at the top would be the groundsheet and tent, with food (if any), canteen, and stove (if any) below; and everything else in the middle. Handy, in case of need, either in the side pockets or conveniently near the top, would be the first-aid outfit, rainwear, sweater, lunch, or anything else wanted *en route*, and the water bucket in case the water supply is on the way to the site. Anything there is no room for inside the rucksack, such as tent or groundsheet, should be strapped on top, not underneath. A frameless rucksack should have nothing hard packed where it will cause the wearer discomfort.

Packing is made much easier by the use of polythene bags. The kit can be grouped into bags – spare clothes, washing, cleaning, storage gear, etc. Spare bags can be taken for keeping separate any soiled or damp articles, cooking utensils or anything else. The bags can be closed with elastic bands or wire fasteners. Squeeze excess air out before sealing.

Pack perishable foods (fats, etc.) and fragile items (eggs, etc.) in the canteen, or plastic, aluminium, or tin containers. Sugar, tea, bread, vegetables, and the like, will pack in polythene bags. Do not use glass containers except as inner linings of other containers.

Practise packing your rucksack. Get it well balanced, and adjusted comfortably high on your back, and take a walk with it.

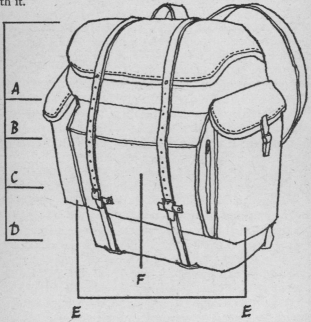

PACKING A RUCKSACK

A *Waterproof* (*coat or cape*) – *Water bucket* – *Groundsheet* – *Tent*
B *Food* (*if any*) – *Canteen* (*or plates*), *mug* – *Stove* (*if any*)
C *Extra clothing* (*sweater, plimsolls, etc.*) – *Spare clothing* (*underwear, socks, etc.*)
D *Sleeping gear* (*sleeping bag, nightwear, etc.*)
E *First-aid gear, matches, torch, etc.* – *Washing gear* (*towel, soap, etc.*)
F *Map* – *Reading or writing material*

18

TENTS

A FIELD of campers today looks very different from what it did only a few years ago. The flood of Continental tents, mainly from France, Germany, Switzerland, and Belgium, has brought new colours, new shapes, and much that is new in poles, groundsheets, fastenings, fly-sheets, and other features. The popular trend is towards frame-tent camping with what the woodcrafter calls luxury equipment, and which requires a car to transport it, but the small-tent camper has not failed to benefit from this Continental invasion.

All Shapes and Sizes

There has always been a wide assortment of tents, chiefly in the smaller sizes. The bigger tents were mostly ridge and bell tents, but they have now been joined by frame and auto tents in their many and varied shapes.

The frame tent first came here from France in 1956. Its main asset is its ample headroom. It comprises a high-walled outer tent rigged over a tubular frame, and strung under it are inner tents varying in number according to the size of the outer tent. There might be several bedrooms, living-room,

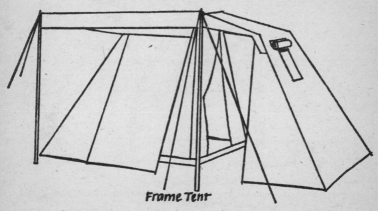

Frame Tent

kitchen, porches, and much else. They range in weight from about 20 to 180 lb, and in price from about £45 to £300.

The auto tent originated from the motorist camper's do-it-yourself improvements to his ridge tent, mainly by extensions to provide for a kitchen or sitting-room, or extra sleeping quarters. The modern manufactured auto tent is usually a one-compartment frame tent with awning, a tent for the touring motorist.

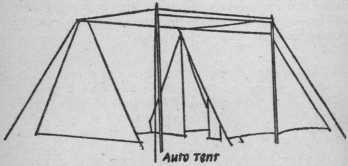

Auto Tent

The pneumatic tent is a poleless igloo-shaped tent. It is erected by inflating the four tubes that run up the sides from the bottom corners to the roof. It first appeared in 1934 and had always been popular with the touring motorist.

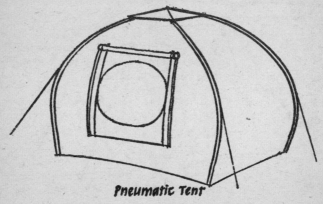

Pneumatic Tent

The bell tent is fast disappearing from the scene. Compared with modern tents there is little to say in its favour. It is usually bought second-hand as ex-army stock, and is too bulky for anything but a van or lorry.

The ridge tent, with its parallel sides and horizontal ridge roof is still one of the commonest shapes of tent, but is becoming less common. The large sizes, 6 or 7 feet high, are now used less for family camping, but are still the first choice for Scout and other youth-movement standing-camps, because of their robustness. A frame tent would have a shorter life in such company.

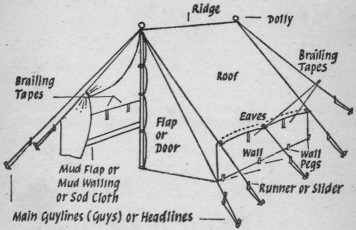

The lightweight tent is either a small ridge tent or a one-pole tent. Some have walls, others not. Both can be fitted with angle-poles to give a clear door space or floor area.

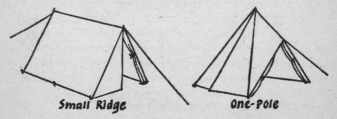

Tent Fabrics

Most tents are made of cotton. Linen, silk, nylon, terylene, and other cloths are used, but cotton remains the leading tent fabric. The chief reasons are that it is comparatively cheap; is in abundant supply; is strong and hard-wearing; and, like other vegetable fibres, is stronger wet than dry.

The Right Weave: Some cheap tents are made from cloth never intended for tent-making. True tent fabric is made from specially selected yarn, closely woven in plain weave, sometimes called basket weave. It is the ideal weave for tents because, in

addition to its strong construction, it permits a tight wind-proof packing of the threads. When wet, the threads swell and pack even tighter, closing up the interstices (spaces where threads cross) and making the cloth waterproof, yet porous to air. Good tent fabrics, therefore, are water-repellent when taken off the loom. Nevertheless, they should always be water-proofed.

Weights: The weight of a tent fabric is stated in ounces per square yard (grammes per square metre for Continental tents) – lightweights from 3 to 5 oz (about 100 to 160 grammes); medium weight from 5 to 8 oz (160 to 270 grammes); heavy-weight from 8 to 12 oz (270 to 400 grammes). Heavier tent fabrics are made, but 12 oz is about the limit for camping.

Cloth Types: Non-cotton cloths generally take the name of the fibre they are made from – silk, nylon, terylene, and they are mostly lightweight fabrics. Cotton cloths get their names from their construction, and sometimes the type of cotton is included. The best cottons, in order of superiority, are Sea Island (rarely used for tents), Egyptian, and American.

The commonest descriptions of cotton tent fabrics are lawn (lightweight), cambric (light and medium weights), duck (medium and heavyweight – to 20 oz and more). Cloth described simply as Egyptian cotton is usually a good quality light or medium weight cloth.

Ventile: This is a medium-weight cotton cloth, air-porous and of superior windproof and water-resistant qualities. It was originally designed for protective clothing for the British soldiers in the heavy rains and heat of Burma during the 1939–45 war. Nowadays it is used for tents and clothing.

Mixture Cloths: These are also called unions, and are usually mixtures of cotton and some other fibre, such as nylon or terylene, to give extra strength.

Colouring: A tent fabric described as vat dyed is likely to be of good quality, because the vat dye is the best of all cotton dyes and the most expensive.

Tent Proofings

All good tent fabrics are waterproofed. Most are also proofed against attack by mildew or rot, or both. Some are also flame-proofed.

Waterproofing: Tent fabrics must be proofed in such a way that they remain air-porous. For that reason, they cannot be made absolutely waterproof. Water-repellent, water-resistant, and similar terms, are more accurate descriptions. A tent made of cloth as waterproof and airtight as a plastic raincoat would drip inside with condensation, whatever the weather.

Mildew: This is a minute fungus which stains, weakens, and finally rots cotton, leather, and other materials. It thrives in warm, moist storage conditions. A mildew-proofed tent is not necessarily rot-proof.

Rot: This is caused by bacteria. They need moister conditions for survival than mildew, and thrive well in damp, warm soil. A rot-proofed tent is usually also proof against mildew.

Fire: Cotton cloth cannot be made fireproof. It can only be made flameproof. Flames spread fire rapidly. A flameproofed cloth burns without flame, and slowly enough to cope with quite easily.

Choosing a Tent

The tent is the most expensive item of a camper's equipment, so care should be taken in choosing the one that is right for the job and that will give good and long service.

We are concerning ourselves here only with lightweight tents (though many of the points made also apply to tents in general) because the choosing and buying of the bigger tents is not normally an individual matter.

What has already been said about the selecting and buying of equipment in general applies to tents in particular, because there are some very poor specimens being sold. There is no point in giving details of dimensions, weights, and prices here, because of the great variety of tents. The suppliers will give you all those details in their latest catalogues. The points given briefly here are to help you make your choice. A good two-man, one-pole tent weighs about 6 lb and costs around £25, at least. A reasonably good two-man ridge tent of about the same weight can be bought at around £12.

Shape, colour, and other details are much a matter of personal preference, but practical reasons should not be overlooked. *Size:* Better a bit big than a bit small. A one-man is lighter than a two-man, but a two-man can be shared with a companion, and so can the weight of the tent as well as other items of equipment.

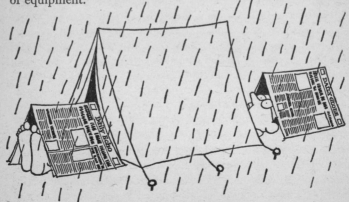

Better a bit big than a bit small

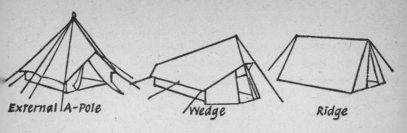

External A-Pole   Wedge   Ridge

One-pole (pyramid, wedge, etc., shape) or ridge tent? The one-pole tent can be pitched single-handed more easily and quickly; size for size it is lighter; its one front guy takes up less ground than the ridge tent's fore and aft guys; it is a more stable shape in wind; weight for weight it is higher and so is more comfortable in bad weather. Reasonably good ridge tents can be bought more cheaply because they are easier to make.

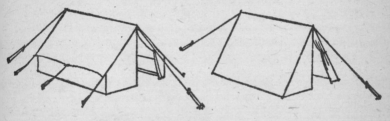

Walls or no walls? A tent without walls costs less and weighs less; it takes up less site space because it has no wall guys; the steep pitch of its roof sheds rain better; and it stands wind better. But it has less headroom and less comfort in bad weather; and there is about 6 inches of unusable floor space all round the inside edge. A tent with walls is more spacious at floor level and above, and to many campers that is worth the extra trouble with guys, wind-gathering eaves, and any other disadvantages. For comfort, the minimum for a two-man ridge tent is about 4 feet 6 inches high and wide, with 18-inch walls.
Which colour? White and bright colours may be pleasant on dull days, but in bright weather they can (unless under a darker-coloured fly-sheet) be uncomfortably glaring, and could keep you awake on a moonlight night. They also attract flying

insects. White soon shows dirt. Tan is a good colour.

Poles: Alloy poles are lighter but dearer than wood. There are some whose sections pack nested into each other. A-poles give a clear floor space to a one-pole tent, and a clear doorway to a ridge tent, but add about 1 lb in weight, and about £3 in cost.

Guys: The synthetic cords, unlike others, do not shrink. Guy tensioners (covered multi-strand elastic) and rubber rings do not require adjustment. Some cord guys have their doubled part at the eaves-end instead of at the peg-end, and a metal ring goes over the peg. This usually puts the runner at a less back-bending height, and the metal ring saves wear and tear of the cord on the peg, and also keeps it out of contact with the

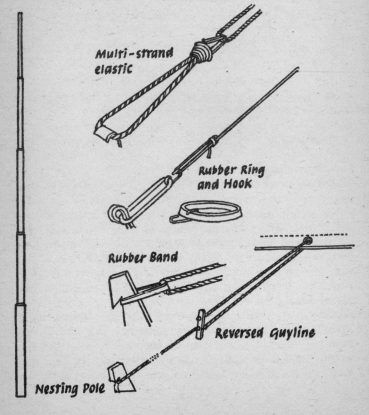

Multi-strand elastic

Rubber Ring and Hook

Rubber Band

Reversed Guyline

Nesting Pole

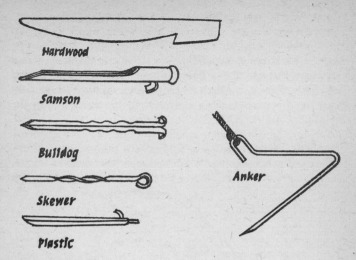

Hardwood

Samson

Bulldog

Anker

Skewer

Plastic

ground. Metal runners save weight and space.

Pegs: Metal pegs are lighter and take up less packing space than wood, and are more easily cleaned and dried. No mallet is needed. There are types for all soils, including the sandiest.

Groundsheets: Plastic (P.V.C., etc.) is better than rubber. It is lighter, and is not affected by age, oil, grease, or flame. A sewn-in groundsheet makes a tent draught-proof and easier to pitch, but the tent cannot be thoroughly aired, and if standing long the ground underneath becomes sour. A sewn-in groundsheet has only one use. A separate groundsheet is a more flexible item. In bad weather it can be folded back to allow anyone entering with muddy boots to take them off before stepping on to the groundsheet. It can be used outside for kit or for sitting on. A cape groundsheet has the one big disadvantage that in bad weather it is often wanted both in the tent and on your back at the same time.

Fly-sheets: These add weight and cost to a tent, nearly as much again of each, but they allow free movement in a tent in wet weather, and the air space between tent and fly-sheet keeps it warmer in cold weather and cooler in warm weather. The fly-sheet should nowhere touch the tent fabric. The down-to-ground type is best. It is not so prone to billowing and provides a shelter for water buckets, muddy boots, firewood, etc. A fly-sheet over external angle-poles can be left up in wet weather while the tent underneath is taken down dry, and vice versa. Polythene fly-sheets are not recommended. In the sun they overheat the tent fabric and can reduce its natural moisture content to such a degree that the fabric eventually tenders and breaks apart.

Bell-ends (useful storage space), peg-out doors, and protective hoods and other refinements, all add to the comfort (and weight and cost) of a tent.

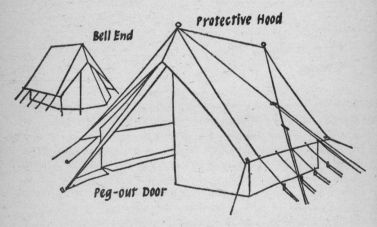

A good tent is built on a framework of pre-shrunk linen tape strengthening its seams, and is reinforced at all points of strain, so necessary to a fine, lightweight fabric. Eaves should be double-ply, and deep enough to shed rain clear of the walls. A tent offered without a sod cloth should be avoided. So should an unproofed tent for serious camping. An unproofed cloth may be water-repellent, but it takes too long to dry out, even after a shower. It is also more likely to be attacked by mildew. A few drops of water swilled round on a proofed cloth will roll about like mercury, without wetting it. Rot-proofing is a further point in a tent's favour.

OTHER GEAR

Rucksacks

There are many ways of carrying your belongings, but for the hiker and lightweight camper the rucksack (a German word meaning 'back sack') is ideal because on the back a load is central and out of the way, and both arms are free.

A rucksack should be waterproof and made of strong fabric, such as rot-proofed cotton duck. For comfort, the shoulder slings should be about 2 inches wide, and of leather or stout webbing. A top flap (hood) with a generous overlap and long fastening straps enables a tent or groundsheet to be packed underneath it when there is no room inside.

Nowadays, most rucksacks are frame-supported. The frame is of a light material such as cane, small-diameter tubular steel or alloy, or flexible steel strip. Some frames are detachable, so that the rucksack can be used 'soft' if desired. The advantages of a frame are that it distributes the pack's weight evenly and transfers part of it to the hips, instead of the shoulders taking it all. And the air space between the pack and the frame keeps the back cool and dry thus lessening the risk of a chill when taken off.

The modern trend in rucksack design (though originated some years ago) is the 'high load' style. It is based on the principle that the human frame can best support a load when it is vertically above the body's centre of gravity, hence the heavy load African women, Billingsgate fish porters, and others, can carry on their heads. The next best thing to balancing your kit on your head is to get it as high as you can in a wedge-shaped bag, wider at the top, and close to the body so that it forms as vertical a line as possible with your spine. In keeping with this principle, most high-load rucksacks have high side pockets; and either no front pocket or one only, intended for a map or other light article.

Frameless

With Frame

High-Pack Design

When buying a rucksack, it is better to choose one a little larger (in bag capacity, not frame size) than a ' comfortable fit' for your kit: it will be easier to pack, more comfortable to wear, and kinder to the rucksack and its contents. Good makes of rucksack are Bergan, B.B. (Brown Best), and Karrimor.

Blankets or Sleeping Bag?

Many new campers start off with blankets borrowed from home and eventually get themselves a sleeping bag.

Blankets for warmth in camp must be all-wool. A blanket with a label describing it as 'blended wool' is best left at home. It is not, as is often thought, an all-wool mixture. It usually contains less than 50% wool, and may legally contain as little as 10%.

To compare blankets for warmth, fold each in the same way – the one which stands the highest is the one to take. With woollen blankets, it is bulk (fluffiness) which gives warmth, not weight.

Sleeping bags are, for several reasons, more suitable than blankets for camping, especially hike-camping. A good sleeping bag giving the same warmth as two good blankets packs much smaller, and weighs less, and saves awkward bed-making in a small tent.

When buying a sleeping bag the chief consideration should be the filling. There are many kinds. Down, the breast feathers of certain ducks and geese, is the best natural filling. It is the warmest, the lightest in weight and packs the smallest. Down and feather mixtures, and curled feathers, come second and third to down.

Terylene (Dacron is the American equivalent) is one of the best synthetic fillings. It is not quite so warm or light as down and does not pack as small, but it is cheaper and, unlike down and feathers, can be washed and drip-dried, and is resistant to moth and mildew. Tricel is similar to Terylene, but is cheaper and inferior to it. Fillings to avoid are kapok, felt, flock, wadding, and such like.

31

A wall- or box-quilted bag gives better insulation than a simple quilted one because it has no through-stitching and so no places without filling. A good bag springs open when untied.

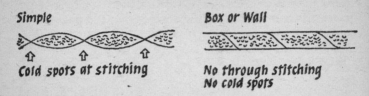

Simple

Cold spots at stitching

Box or Wall

No through stitching
No cold spots

A tapered-shape bag is warmer to the feet than a rectangular shape, but a rectangular-shaped convertible bag can be unzipped to form a bed quilt for use at home.

A washable sheet inner-lining keeps a bag clean, protects the fabric from soiling by body oils, and prolongs its life.

Study the catalogues of the reputable suppliers before making your choice, then buy the very best you can afford.

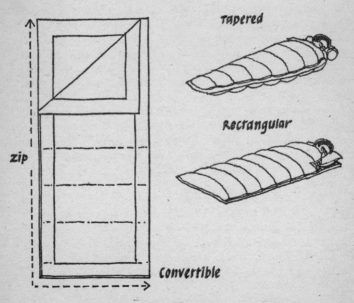

Tapered

Rectangular

zip

Convertible

Cooking and Other Gear

There is a wide choice of cooking utensils. They are mostly in compact sets comprising anything from three to eight or more items, nesting ingeniously one into another and designed to take up as little space as possible. A typical two-man lightweight set is the Cookwell canteen made up of a 2-pint saucepan, a frypan, and a plate or lid, and weighing 16 oz. Heavy-gauge aluminium is the best for the lightweight camper cooking on an open fire. Lighter weights are more suitable for cooking stoves.

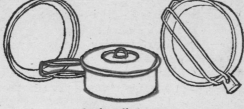

Cookwell Canteen

Cooking pots should be round and seamless. The wider the base, the quicker the cooking. Detachable handles make cleaning easier. Paint-pot pattern billies, especially nesting sets, are very useful for bigger numbers, but those with handles not designed to stay upright (away from the flames) should be avoided.

Nesting Billies

Water Containers: Buckets and washbowls can be obtained in canvas or plastic. The wedge-shaped (wider at the base) stand up better than the straight-sided. Canvas and plastic (P.V.C.) are about the same in weight – 1-gallon bucket – 3 oz. Canvas must be saturated before it becomes watertight, and so cannot be dried as quickly as plastic. There are also collapsible water carriers. They pack small and cost little. One 1-gallon model on sale has a watertight cap, weighs 4 oz and costs 35p.

Polythene Water Carriers

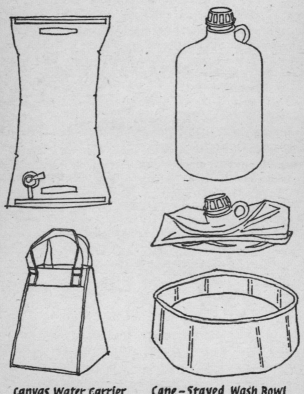

Canvas Water Carrier   Cane-Stayed Wash Bowl

Buying Equipment

With the growing popularity of camping, and especially the boom in family camping, many new firms have sprung into being to supply the increased demand for equipment. Some of these firms know little about camping. They copy the goods of established manufacturers, particularly the software such as tents, rucksacks, and sleeping bags, using inferior and sometimes totally unsuitable materials, and offer them at a lower price. This kind of equipment is a waste of money, quite apart from what it can do to a camp or hike.

How can the inexperienced camper or hiker be expected to know which equipment can be relied on? He cannot, but the next best thing is to know which suppliers can be relied on. He will not go far wrong if he buys only from firms with an established reputation for good quality and service, such as Blacks of Greenock, Bukta, Briggs, Pindisports, and Scout Shops; and from the newer firms whose equipment has been recommended by satisfied customers.

Most suppliers invite you to send for their catalogues. Get them and browse through them. Try to see and handle what appeals to you, in shops or showrooms, or at one of the many exhibitions held these days; better still, see equipment in actual use and get the opinions of users.

When you decide to buy an item of equipment, aim at getting the best for your particular needs (which does not necessarily mean the most expensive) even if you have to wait until you can afford it.

On the way

FINDING your way by map and compass for the first time, enjoying a meal in the open, and arriving back from your hike on two comfortable feet, gives you the pleasurable satisfaction of having achieved something worth while. You feel a little more self-sufficient and self-reliant. A night in a tent, well-fed, warm, and weatherproof, in spite of the rain, is just as gratifying.

Hiking and camping are in themselves great fun, but they are even greater fun and more enduring when they are a means to something else. For example, if you have an interest or hobby that you can combine with your hiking or camping, such as bird- or animal-watching, angling, photography, sketching, butterflies or moths, or brass rubbings, you can do the two together and enjoy the pleasure of them both at the same time. Here are some hike suggestions. Camp can be a good base for many of them.

Photographers and sketchers can 'collect' inn signs, weather vanes, windmills, watermills, sundials, churchyard or market crosses, church lych gates or sanctuary knockers, bridges, types of stile or gate, or gate fastenings, village relics such as stocks, whipping posts, ducking stools, pillories, gibbets, lock-ups, pumps, bull rings, or fire engines.

Nature enthusiasts can collect specimens, or visit special sites, or nature reserves, bird sanctuaries, heronries, or aviaries. A television feature or play, or a film or book, might suggest a hike to the scene of it – a village, historic ruins, the site of a battle.

The Ordnance Survey maps of Monastic Britain, Roman Britain, Anglo-Saxon, and other periods, offer lots of ideas for short or several-day hikes or expeditions of exploration, following ancient trackways and locating settlements. And also, for the historically minded, there is no shortage of castles, abbeys, moot-halls, old churches, and cathedrals.

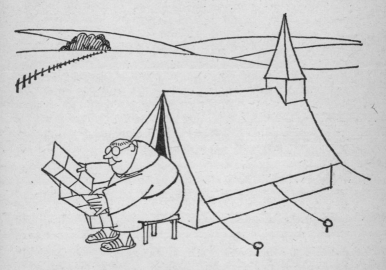

For the scientifically minded, the countryside is the location of a variety of installations, some of which are open to the public at certain times, or are almost as interesting to see from the outside – weather stations, observatories, radio transmitters, nuclear power stations, radio telescopes, satellite tracking stations, airfields. There are also museums of motor-cars, traction engines, aircraft, and the like.

Other ideas for hikes or expeditions include reconnoitring a site or area and reporting on its suitability for a standing camp; a bee-line hike, entailing walking on a single compass bearing across open country to arrive at a specified point; following a stream to its source; a curiosity hike – go and see for yourself a trigonometrical point (triangulation station) or a place with an odd name, such at The Pludds, Land of Nod, Great Snoring, Pity Me, Christmas Pie; locate some puzzling feature or unexplained symbol on a map – but not something non-existent, like the cross denoting a longitude–latitude intersection. There is also the star-navigation hike (on a clear, moonless night), and the moonlight hike. Observing natural clues to direction (north pointers) and checking them with a compass can be a useful and interesting *en route* activity on most types of hike.

Inquire at your local public library (reference section) for details and locations of places you may be interested in, and (where applicable) days and times of opening and so avoid a disappointment on arrival. They may also have the published list of country places where village crafts are still carried on, and details of country fairs, carnivals, traditional ceremonies, customs quaint to the stranger, and other annual or special happenings which may add interest to a hike.

THE OPEN ROAD

WHETHER you are setting out on a camping hike, or on a day hike from home or from camp, make sure you have everything you planned to take and that everything is complete (no tent pegs missing), and check with each other any items you have agreed to share, otherwise you may discover too late that you have no matches and two first-aid outfits instead.

Walking: Foot comfort is more important to the walker than anything else. Feet stuck into unfamiliar shoes or boots of heavier weight than usual and made to walk in them much farther then usual are not happy feet, as their owner soon discovers. Feet must be allowed gradually to get used to the unfamiliar.

A few local walks will break-in new footwear and help to harden soft feet and make them more blister-proof. The ideal is to be wearing your rucksack packed as for the hike. You can then get that comfortably settled too, packed evenly balanced and not pulling more on one shoulder than the other.

The feet can be hardened by applying methylated or surgical spirit, or by soaking them in hot water with plenty of common salt and a little bicarbonate of soda. Better still, they can be hardened naturally by going barefoot about the house or garden.

On the road, wear one or two pairs of fairly thick woollen stockings. One pair can be over-socks turned down over the shoe tops to keep stones out.

A good foot drill for a several-day hike is to wash the feet daily, dry thoroughly, and dust feet and inside stockings with talcum or boracic powder. Keep the nails short, cut straight across, not rounded. Carry at least two pairs of spare stockings with you and wash and change them frequently. Washing keeps wool soft. Even on a day hike carry a spare pair. They can save you a blister if you get a hole in the pair you are wearing, as well as freshening the feet up.

If you do get a blister, prick it at the side in two places, press out the fluid, and apply a sterile adhesive strip dressing.

Dubbin or oil (mars oil) your boots or shoes occasionally, and treat with polish frequently. Wet boots or shoes should never be heat-dried: it will ruin them. Stuff them with paper, cloth, grass, or the like. This absorbs the moisture and helps them keep their shape.

Distance: Do not tackle more than you have prepared yourself for. You will be spoiling your own fun. If you are quite new to hiking, start with easy afternoon or evening jaunts of 5 or 6 miles (about 2 hours' walking), carrying in your rucksack no more than a sweater, rainwear, first-aid kit, and perhaps sandwiches and a flask. Work up to full-day hikes of 10 to 15 miles, travelling light; then later taking a canteen and perhaps a stove, and cooking yourself a meal. The next stage is a weekend camp, carrying all your gear about 5 miles; then gradually improving on the distance until you can comfortably average 10 miles a day from site to site, over a period of a week or more, and making 12 miles the maximum for any one day.

Planning and routine: Long-term hikes must be planned ahead so that likely camp sites will be within your average daily mileage. Some hikers book their sites in advance. This saves time finding sites daily, but it prevents you changing your plans once you have started out.

It is usual to make a gentle start on the first day or two to get into your swing, and also to have an occasional half day in camp for a rest, airing kit or drying out, and any necessary repairs. Some prefer to stay longer on a site and to hike out from it, travelling light, and returning each night.

Routine varies according to circumstances. For example, on a sunny morning after a wet night an early start might advisedly be postponed to allow wet and heavy tents to be dried out.

Adopt your own routine and try to keep to it. You will be fitter as a result. Aim always at getting a good night's sleep, turning in no later than you do at home; and at having regular meals, as near as possible to your normal times. Start the day with a good breakfast. Rest for an hour after the midday meal. Light nourishing meals are better than heavy stodgy ones.

A steady, even pace makes walking easier. A common hike routine is to walk 50 minutes, then to rest 10 minutes with your rucksack off and, if possible, lying on your back (on something waterproof) with your feet up. During stops put a sweater on, unless in the sun. Walking in the sun, protect head, neck, arms, and other parts not normally exposed.

Arrive in each site area with at least enough time to find a site, pitch camp, settle in, and cook and eat a meal in good light.

It is a wise precaution to have with you enough money for the fare home from the most distant point of your hike.

The Cycle-camper

Apart from the packing and carrying of kit and equipment, cycle-camping is basically the same as any other form of lightweight camping. If, as the hike-camper may think, the cyclist is at a disadvantage having to keep to the roads, he makes up for it by being able to travel faster and farther, and in not being dependent on the nearness of shops when he chooses a camp site.

Here are some points which may be helpful to the new cyclecamper.

The Cycle: Be sure that it is fully equipped, completely roadworthy, and that you take your tools and repair outfit. Both brakes should be really effective because of the extra weight.

Keep your tyres hard (it makes riding easier) and check regularly for embedded flints. The back wheel will be the better for having tandem-type heavy-gauge spokes.

For a comfortable riding position, let the saddle and the handlebars take the weight of your body equally. Have the height of your handle bar grips no more than 3 or 4 inches above or below the height of your saddle. With the peak of the saddle 2 or 3 inches behind the line of the bottom bracket, your arms should be slightly bent when you grip the handlebars. Your knees should also be slightly bent when the pedals are at their lowest point.

Packing: All your kit and equipment should be carried on your cycle, in panniers, saddle bag, and on carriers. This keeps the weight nearer to the ground and makes for steadier and safer riding. Never carry anything on yourself. A rucksack on your back, as well as being unnecessarily tiring, can easily upset your balance and your steering.

The back carrier should be of lightweight tubular steel, and of a design which keeps the panniers clear of the wheel. The carrier stays should grip the back fork firmly enough to prevent any jogging of the load forcing them down. Carriers with stays long enough to bolt on to the wheel spindle cannot slip.

Whether you buy panniers, or use Army-type packs, fix them so that they will not slip backwards or forwards, or swing outwards when cornering. Most of the load will be at the back, but it is advisable to have some weight at the front (though not enough to affect the steering – small panniers or handlebar bag) to hold the wheel down when travelling uphill. Front panniers or bags can be dangerous if not firmly fixed and budge-proof.

When packing your kit, follow the same principle as for packing a rucksack – put in first what you will need last. Pack always in the same way, and keep associated articles together – sleeping bag, nightwear, and spare clothes; tent, groundsheet, and pegs; stove, windscreen, paraffin; canteen, etc.; and so on. Keep handy anything likely to be wanted *en route*. For safety aim at a low, securely packed load with the weight of the panniers as near equal as possible.

Keep the weight of your kit and equipment down by taking only what you really need, and sharing mutual items such as tentage and cooking gear.

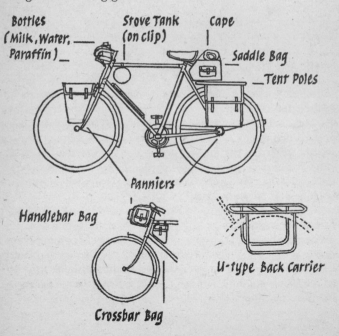

Clothing: Shorts, a zip-fronted, showerproof jacket, long stockings, and light shoes, are suitable wear. The shorts are better woollen than cotton. The jacket should be hip-length and loose-fitting enough for a sweater or two to be worn underneath when needed. For rain – slip-over cape, sou'wester, and leggings.

The Country Code

Most of us will be more familiar with the Highway Code than the Country Code. The Highway Code was compiled by the Ministry of Transport with the purpose of making our roads safer and reducing the number of accidents. The Country Code was compiled by the National Parks Commission, and has as its aim the preservation of the beauty and order of the countryside. Like the Highway Code, it is a code of conduct based on good manners and good sense. Every hiker and camper worthy of the name sees to it that he knows the few simple rules of the code and strictly observes them. The thoughtless or selfish act can cause serious harm to the countryside and wild life, as well as to the goodwill of the country folk on which the hiker and camper so much depend.

Guard against all risk of fire
Fires started by matches and cigarette-ends thoughtlessly thrown away, or pipes carelessly knocked out; camp or picnic fires not properly put out; and broken bottles acting as burning glasses in the sun, do much costly damage every year to crops, haystacks, forest plantations, woodlands, and heaths. Stamp or beat out, if you can, any fire you discover. If you cannot, report to the police or fire brigade as soon as possible.

Fasten all gates
Straying animals can damage crops or injure themselves. Loose on a road, there is greater danger still. Gates obviously intended to be left open, for example, to allow animals to get to a trough, should be left as found. Such gates are usually standing wide open.

Keep dogs under proper control

More harm is done to farm animals by dogs than by any other single cause. Even the small friendly dog chasing animals just for fun can do as much harm as a big fierce dog. A strange dog among cattle, sheep, or poultry can be frightening or disturbing enough to cause a calf or a lamb to be born dead, or for a cow to give less milk, or for poultry to be put off their lay.

Keep to the paths across farmland

Crops, including standing grass, are damaged by trampling at any stage of their growth. Walking in single file on field paths which have crops on either side spares the crops and also keeps the path well defined.

Avoid damaging fences, hedges, and walls

Use stiles and gates. Don't force your way through fences or hedges, or knock walls down. Where you had got through, animals might follow. Don't climb over gates unless you must, and then keep to the hinged end to avoid strain on the gate or the fastening.

Leave no litter

Litter, as well as being unsightly, can be dangerous. Tins and bottles can injure animals and damage farm machinery. Picnickers should take litter away with them. If they have to leave it behind, they should bury it, not throw it into streams or ditches. It should be buried deep enough to prevent foxes or dogs nosing it out and unearthing it.

Safeguard water supplies

Many country people depend on wells and streams for water for themselves and their animals. Take care not to foul or interfere with their water supplies in any way.

Protect wild life, wild flowers and trees

Take care to avoid disturbing or injuring wild life. Tree branches should not be broken or torn off, or their bark slashed or carved. Flowers give more pleasure to more people if they

44

are left growing. Birds and their eggs, animals, plants, and trees should be left alone.

Go carefully on country roads
If there is no footpath, walkers are generally safer on the right of the road, facing oncoming traffic. Where there is an adequate footpath, use it. When crossing a country road see that you have a clear view both ways. Avoid crossing where the view is limited, as on the brow of a hill, or near a bend, or approaching a humpback bridge.

Respect the life of the countryside
To the countryman much of the countryside is an outdoor workshop, the place of business where he earns his living. Many of his working tools, such as tractor and plough, and much of his stock and supplies, have to be left out in the open within sight and reach of everybody. Costly damage is often done. Those who respect his property leave it alone and do nothing to interfere with his work or his livelihood. Country people usually keep earlier hours than townspeople, especially in summer, their busiest time. So, cut down the noise at night, particularly in villages. Live and let live.

Hikers and Campers and the Law

Most footpaths shown on a 1-inch Ordnance Survey map are public, but (as is stated at the foot of the map) the representation of a road, track, or footpath is no evidence of the existence of a right of way. Many footpaths give no indication whether they are public or not, while some brandish a warning notice that trespassers will be prosecuted. So, what is the hiker to do?

An unmarked footpath can reasonably be assumed to be public unless it obviously runs only as far as a farm or house, or the like.

Notices warning that trespassers will be prosecuted (except

Warning notices are meaningless

those put up by public authorities such as railways, government departments, and the police) are meaningless and can be ignored. They were once legal, but are no longer so. So long as you keep to the path, do no damage, and strictly observe the Country Code, there is nothing to fear from this kind of warning sign, which has been described as the Wooden Liar.

Should you find yourself being ordered off a path you thought was public, you must leave at once, but the Law requires that you be permitted to proceed to the nearest public way. You cannot be forced to return by the way you came, if that is the greater distance, so apologize (you are in the wrong) and depart.

Campers may not legally camp anywhere at all without permission. Even mountains and moorland belong to somebody or some authority, and though objection is seldom raised, it is common courtesy to inquire at any nearby house or farm whether their permission is required.

MAP AND COMPASS

THE map and the compass are great mysteries to many people, but there is nothing mysterious about either of them. They are both fairly easy to understand. A map is a kind of picture of the ground as seen from above, and a compass is a pointer that tells you which way round to hold the map so that you can find your way about with it.

A map and compass are invaluable tools of the traveller in the countryside. Learn how to use them and they will serve you well.

Compasses

The earliest magnetic compasses were nothing more than a magnetized needle floating on a reed on water. The mysterious magnetic force which causes compass needles to align themselves roughly north to south is still not satisfactorily explained. Today, the types and variety of compasses are almost unlimited.

All compasses have two things in common – a magnetic needle and a card showing the compass points. The cheaper compasses have a fixed card with the needle balanced above it on a pivot. Better ones have the card itself balanced on the pivot, the needle being fixed underneath. Others have the card floating in a heavy liquid so that it quickly comes to rest.

Some compasses have a special attachment for sighting objects and taking accurate bearings, such as the prism on a prismatic compass, and the reflector on some other types. They enable the user to see both the object and the compass reading at eye level. A fairly new introduction is the Silva compass. It is a compass mounted on a rectangular, protractor-like base. It is accurate and easier to use than most.

For ordinary map reading a compass need not be expensive. The cheapest reliable compass is the round type costing about 50p. The type with needle and compass card combined is easier to use than fixed card type, because the free-swinging card does not require the whole compass to be turned to bring the needle over the north point. A compass is also the better for having a hinged lid for protecting the glass and also (usually) automatically checking needle movement when closed.

Using a Compass

Before using a compass to find direction or to take a bearing, make sure that there are no magnetic materials near enough to deflect the compass needle, such as a knife in your pocket, rucksack frame, wire fencing, cycle, motor vehicles, railway lines, or other steel or ironwork.

Hold the compass level so that the needle or card is clear of the glass, and swinging freely.

The Service-type prismatic compass is perhaps the most useful and accurate of all compasses, though it is rather heavy and cumbersome for ordinary map reading. There are several other types, but they are all similar in principle.

To use a prismatic compass, open the lid at right angles (as shown) and turn the prism over as far as it will go. Put your thumb (pointing towards the lid) through the ring and rest the compass on your forefinger.

Raise the prism to your eye and hold the compass level. Sight the object with the hair (or scribe) line cutting vertically through its centre, then read off the bearing by noting through the prism the number of degrees under the bottom of the hair-line.

Other compasses with mirrors or reflectors, such as the better Silva types, can be operated in a similar way to the prismatic compass.

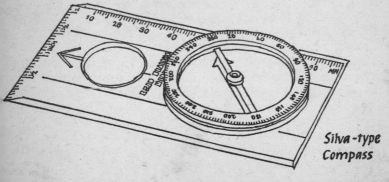

Silva-type
Compass

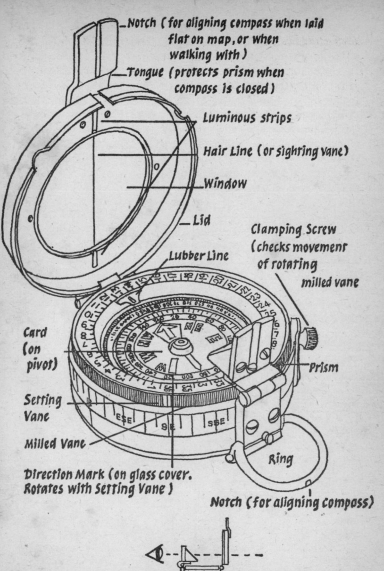

Notch (for aligning compass when laid flat on map, or when walking with)

Tongue (protects prism when compass is closed)

Luminous strips

Hair Line (or sighting Vane)

Window

Lid

Clamping Screw (checks movement of rotating milled vane

Lubber Line

Card (on pivot)

Setting Vane

Milled Vane

Prism

Ring

Direction Mark (on glass cover. Rotates with Setting Vane)

Notch (for aligning compass)

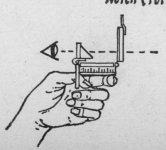

Magnetic variation: Owing to the magnetic poles not coinciding with the true pole, the magnetic attraction in the British Isles (it varies throughout the world, and even within the British Isles) causes the compass needle to lie in a line about 10° west of true north. This is called Magnetic Variation of Declination of the Compass, and should be allowed for when using a compass. The exact allowance to make is shown on o.s. maps, along with the date. This is necessary because the variation is decreasing by about half a degree in four years. This fact is also stated at the foot of o.s. maps.

Compass Bearings

When we talk about the bearing of an object, we mean its direction. But direction in relation to what? There must be a known reference point, in the same way that the distance to a place must be measured from some known point if it is to have any meaning.

The point to which all bearings are related is the north line, and they are measured from it in a clockwise direction. So, when we say that the bearing of an object is 45°, we mean that it is 45° of arc in a clockwise direction from north.

There are three north points from which bearings can be measured – magnetic north, as taken with a compass when finding the magnetic bearing of an object on the ground; grid north, when ascertaining the grid bearing of an object on the map; and true north, for stating the true bearing of an object on the ground.

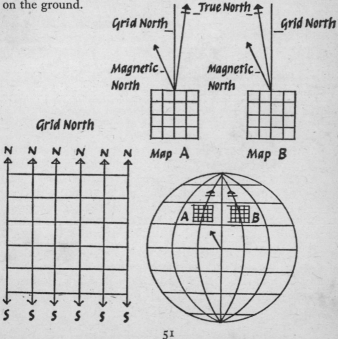

Why take bearings? Map makers, surveyors, and the like, take bearings chiefly for plotting (recording on paper) the positions of objects. Map users, when they take bearings, either do so to find on a map something they can see on the ground, in which case they would take a magnetic bearing and convert it to a grid bearing; or to find on the ground an object they can see on the map, when they would take a grid bearing from the map, convert it, and locate the object by compass.

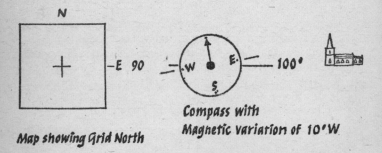

Map showing Grid North

Compass with Magnetic variation of 10° W

Map bearing of church = 90°; compass bearing = 100°. Where magnetic variation is westerly (as in the British Isles) the compass always overstates (by 10° here), so:

(a) Deduct the variation to convert a compass bearing to a map (grid) bearing. (b) Add the variation to a map bearing to convert it to a compass bearing.

If you wish to know the bearing of your own position from an object, there is no need to go to the object to take the bearing. It can be calculated by taking the bearing of the object and adding 180° to it if the result does not exceed 360°. If it does, you deduct 180°. This is called a back bearing. Example: forward bearing 45° – back bearing 225°; forward bearing 200° – back bearing 20°.

Bearings taken for accurate compass work are always stated in degrees, because a reading can be given to the nearest 360th part of the compass card. For ordinary map reading, the named compass points serve well enough. Even a half of the 32 is adequate.

Maps – understanding them

A map can be defined as a flat representation of the whole or a part of the earth's surface or of the heavens. When an area represented is very small, such as a farmstead or town centre, and is drawn in large detail, the reproduction is called a plan. A sea map, as used by navigators and others, is known as a chart.

Many and varied as maps are, they all have one common purpose – to give information.

The hiker in unfamiliar country wants a map that will give him information about his surroundings. He wants to be able to find his own way, and to vary his route to suit himself. He may wish to take a short cut or to by-pass a town, or to avoid main roads and keep to footpaths, or to go off exploring some feature on the ground or on the map that takes his fancy.

The map for the hiker, cyclist, or any other traveller, is the topographical map. The word topography means a description (graphos) of a place (topos). Whereas some maps give only specially selected information, such as the Ordnance Survey map of Britain in the Dark Ages, and the Gas and Coke map of communications and depots, the topographical map gives a detailed description of the area it covers. It presents a general picture, showing all the natural and man-made features – hills and dales, roads and rivers, churches and windmills, and as much else of the permanent fixtures of town and country as scale permits.

With the right map and an understanding of it, you can get about in strange country as easily as you would with a friend who knew it well. In effect, your map is such a friend as that. It is a friend with much information to give. It gives it in language of its own, but it is fairly easy to learn and to understand, and the more of it you know the more information you will get.

Mapping has some special words of its own, but like other specialized vocabularies most of the difficult-looking words have quite simple meanings. When a botanist, for instance, says campanulate, he simply means bell-shaped, and when you break your arm the doctor tells you that you have fractured your humerus. As map reading is something you do, rather than something you write or read about, you can forget most of the technical terms once you have grasped their meaning.

The four basic essentials of good map-reading are: an understanding of scale (including the vertical – contours); orientation (map setting with or without compass, and north points); conventional signs; and the reference system (for stating or locating position). Let us, for a general understanding of these essentials, look at them in the elementary form in which they must so often have appeared on rough sketch maps made (without any knowledge of the map maker's art or terminology) simply by setting down the details essential to the particular purpose. Many such maps have been associated with hidden treasure, so our elementary map maker will be the notorious pirate, Dead-eye Finnigan.

Dead-eye rows alone to a small desert island to bury a casket. The island is circular with a solitary palm tree standing in the middle. Dead-eye stands at the tree and looks for a landmark. There is none, but a little way out to sea there is a small rock. He faces the rock, walks twenty paces and there buries the casket, leaving no trace of where it is hidden. Then on a piece of parchment the pirate draws a circle to represent the island, and in the middle of it he does a drawing of the palm tree. At about the right distance from his tree he puts a cross to show where the casket is buried, and beside it he writes '20 paces from the tree'. (1)

So far, so good, but Dead-eye sees a snag. He may not be able to return for the casket himself. He may have to send his trusty shipmate, Peg-leg Peters. If Peg-leg came to the tree with the map, how could he know which way to face with it so that the position of the cross would give the correct direction for pacing to the hidden casket? (in other words, how could he ORIENTATE or SET the map?)

Dead-eye solves this problem by adding to his map the rock. So now, Peg-leg would only have to face the rock and turn the map until its tree and rock were in line with the real tree and rock. The cross would then give the correct position of the casket. (This is setting a map by landmarks – the tree and the rock.) (2)

But Dead-eye sees another snag. Peg-leg's pace is shorter than his. He would start digging in the wrong place. It is clear to Dead-eye that the means of measuring the distance from the tree must be the same for him and Peg-leg, and for any other trusty shipmate who may use the map. Conveniently, Dead-eye has in his boat a length of rope knotted at 1-foot intervals. And in his pocket he has an old ship halfpenny which, like all other old ship halfpennies measures exactly 1 inch across. With the rope he finds that the island measures 100 yards across, and with the help of the halfpenny as a measure he redraws his map, making the island 10 inches across. In the bottom margin he writes '1 inch to 10 yards'. Then he accurately measures the distance he had already paced out to the spot where the casket is buried, rubs the cross off the map and the wording saying the spot is twenty paces from the tree, and puts in a new cross 2 inches from the tree and without any wording. (The map is now drawn to SCALE. The scale is 1 inch to 10 yards. One inch on the map equals 10 yards on the ground, and the distance between any two points anywhere on the island is in the same proportion. Dead-eye has put the cross 2 inches from the map tree, which means that the casket is buried 20 yards from the real tree.)

Dead-eye, knowing that Peg-leg would be likely to arrive at the island without a halfpenny or other means of measuring map distances, draws a 6-inch horizontal line in the bottom margin, marks it off in inches and then divides the first inch into smaller parts (This is called a SCALE LINE, or simply a 'scale' when it is not likely to be confused with the other meaning of scale already given.) (3)

While Dead-eye has been busying himself, the water level has been rising and the rock has now disappeared. Dead-eye, realizing that the rock cannot always be relied on, must find some other way of setting the map. Had the island been pear-shaped, Peg-leg could have set the map by turning it to 'fit' the island, but the island is circular. Dead-eye looks at the sun. He knows that when it is at its highest in the sky, it is due south and shadows are at their shortest. The sun happens to be due south and therefore the palm tree's shadow is at its shortest and pointing north. So he sets the map and draws an arrow on it pointing in the same direction as the north shadow. Now, Peg-leg had only to find north and point the arrow at it, and the map is set. (The map now has a TRUE NORTH point.) (4)

Clouds are beginning to gather and Dead-eye wonders how Peg-leg would set the map without landmarks or the sun. Then he remembers the compass he has in the boat and fetches it. He stands at the tree with his compass and faces the tree's shadow. Allowing for the shadow's slight move away from true north since he put the north point on the map, Dead-eye notes that the compass needle points about 10° to the west of true north. This is what he had expected, and he adds another arrow to the true north arrow to show anybody setting the map by compass what allowance to make to find true north. (Now,

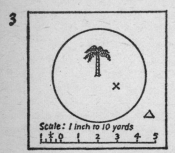

the map has a MAGNETIC NORTH point. The difference between true north and magnetic north is called the MAGNETIC VARIATION.) (5)

Dead-eye is well pleased with his map and with the island, and decides this is a good place for future buryings. But there is a problem. How could he let Peg-leg know the position of any small area of the island when he was away and could only send him written instructions telling him where he wanted him to dig? Dead-eye looks at the map and ponders. The answer is to divide the map into small squares, number them, and make an exact copy of the map for Peg-leg. Then, Dead-eye would only need to refer to a number and Peg-leg could locate the position from his own map.

While Dead-eye is studying his map, before starting to make the copy, it occurs to him that the picture of the palm tree will take up too much space now that there are to be more buryings marked on the map, and will surely get in the way. So he rubs out the picture and puts in its place a symbol of his own invention. Then he enters the same symbol in the bottom margin and writes 'Palm Tree' beside it so that anybody else using the map will know what the symbol stands for. (Symbols on maps are called CONVENTIONAL SIGNS.) (6)

Dead-eye finishes the copy map and divides both maps into squares, but he decides against numbering the squares because a whole square would be too big an area. He wants to be able to narrow the area down to be more certain of locating things buried. Instead, he numbers the lines, horizontal and vertical,

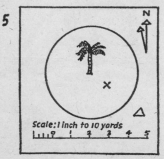

5

Scale: 1 inch to 10 yards

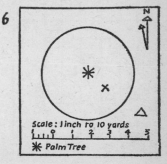

6

Scale: 1 inch to 10 yards

✳ Palm Tree

and starts the numbering at the bottom left-hand corner. For Peg-leg's benefit, he writes out a separate explanation. He tells him that to give a position he simply notes how far eastwards it is from the bottom left-hand corner, then how far northwards, and writes down the two results as one. He gives as an example the position of the cross where the casket is buried. He tells him the position is 4A2C, and to find it he would start at the bottom left-hand corner and run his finger eastwards until it was level with the cross, just past line 4. Peg-leg was to imagine the space between lines as being divided into three parts, called A, B, and C. He would note the eastward distance as 4A, then move his finger northward to 2C and write the position as 4A2C. He warned Peg-leg that he must always state the eastward distance first, or the position would be wrong. Horizontal first, he told him, then vertical – like a monkey running to a tree and climbing it. The position of the palm tree, he added, was 3B3B. (Any method of referring to a position on a map is called a MAP REFERENCE SYSTEM. The framework of squares on a map is called a GRID. A map reference system based on a grid, like Dead-eye's and that of most maps, is called a GRID REFERENCE SYSTEM. The group of figures which give a position is called a MAP REFERENCE or a GRID REFERENCE. The two parts which make up the reference are called the CO-ORDINATES. The first part is known as the EASTING, and the second part as the NORTHING. The co-ordinates forming Dead-eye's grid reference for the position

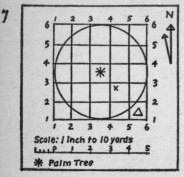

Scale: 1 inch to 10 yards

* Palm Tree

of the casket were 4A – the easting, and 2C – the northing, written as 4A2C.) (7)

Now that we know something about a map's chief ingredients, and have an idea what most of the technical terms mean, let us leave Dead-eye on his island (until we return to consider contours) and take a practical look at map reading.

Your Map

The best map for the walker is the Ordnance Survey map on a scale of 1 inch to 1 mile, better known to its friends as the 1-inch o.s. map. There are 190 sheets of it, covering the whole of Great Britain. Each sheet bears a number and the name of a place or district (Hastings, North York Moors, etc.), and represents an area about 25 miles from west to east, and 28 miles from north to south. They can be bought at most bookshops or borrowed from bigger public libraries, and are usually mounted on cloth, folded and in covers. This 'style' is called 'mounted folded'. There are cheaper styles – paper flat, and paper folded. An index of all the sheets is on the back cover of 1-inch o.s. maps. When buying or borrowing a map, you need to state scale, sheet number or name, and style.

Nowadays, with so much new building and road-making in progress, maps soon become out of date. So it is wise to consider, before buying a new map, how much use it is likely to get. A map case will prolong the life of a paper map, but for frequent use the cloth-mounted map, folded and in covers, can be the cheapest in the long run. Maps are always being revised. The latest 1-inch o.s. edition is the Seventh Series. Do not buy an earlier edition than this if you want the best value for your 50p or so. The 1-inch series is now being replaced by a new series in a slightly larger scale – 1:50000, which is about $1\frac{1}{4}$ inches to one mile. At present, only maps of half of Britain are available (south of an east-west line through Lancaster); the northern half is to be published in 1976.

The Scale

Scale is the proportion that a distance between any two points on a map bears to the distance between the same two points on the ground. We already know enough about scale to be able to understand this. Scale has much to do with the amount of detail a map can show. Imagine yourself in a rising helicopter with a foot-square glass panel in its floor. The view through the panel will look like a square picture of the ground below. The higher you rise, the more ground will appear in the picture and the smaller the detail will become. Everything, in fact, is on a smaller scale. It is the same with maps. The bigger the area represented on a given size of map sheet, the smaller the scale and the amount of detail.

The 1-inch map, which is classified as a small scale map, is the best map for the walker because the scale is small enough to cover a fair-sized area (about 700 square miles each map sheet) and not too small (but almost) to show the kind of detail he wants. On a scale less than 1 inch to 1 mile it is not possible to show footpaths, byways, antiquities, or similar useful detail. The standard cycling map is the $\frac{1}{2}$-inch (2 miles to 1 inch), because of the greater area it covers.

The scale of a map can be shown in three ways: in words – 'one inch to one mile'; by the scale line at the foot of the map; and by the Representative Fraction, commonly known as the R.F. The scale of 1 inch to 1 mile can be written as a fraction by turning the mile into inches – 1/63360, there being 63,360 inches in a mile. The R.F. of Dead-eye's map, which had a scale of 1 inch to 10 yards, would be 1/360. The advantage of showing a map scale as an R.F. is that any unit of measure can be applied to it – centimetres, inches, feet – so long as both parts of the fraction are expressed in the same unit. For example, to a Frenchman with Dead-eye's map, inches and feet might mean nothing, but if the R.F. were shown, he would (if he knew about scales) measure on the map the distance from the tree to the cross in centimetres, then for each centimetre he would measure 360 centimetres along the ground and arrive at the right spot. A comparison between the R.F. of a

1-inch map and Dead-eye's shows clearly that the smaller the denominator the larger the scale. If you picked up a Continental map with an R.F. of 1/50,000 (likely to be written 1 : 50 000) you would know, comparing it with our 1-inch R.F., that the scale was about 1¼ inches to the mile.

Ground as seen through floor of rising helicopter

View 2 miles square (scale: 1 inch to 1 mile)

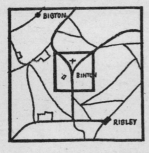

View 8 miles square (scale: 4 miles to 1 inch)

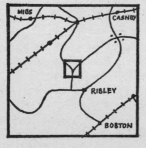

View 20 miles square (scale: 10 miles to 1 inch)

Contours

Contour lines are a means of showing hills and dales, heights and slopes, and other features of relief, on the flat surface of a map. There are other methods, and some of them are used along with contours to give a clearer picture of the terrain they represent. Two such are shading, and layer tinting – the use of colours for different heights.

The contour system, as well as being the most accurate method of representing relief, is the most suitable because, being a system of lines only, it hardly interferes with other detail on the map. The lines indicate height above sea level, and the difference in height between one line and the next is (on 1-inch o.s. maps) 50 feet. So, a contoured map can be said to have two scales – one for the horizontal distances and another for the vertical. On the 2½-inch o.s. map the difference in height between adjacent contour lines (called the v.i. – Vertical Interval) is 25 feet.

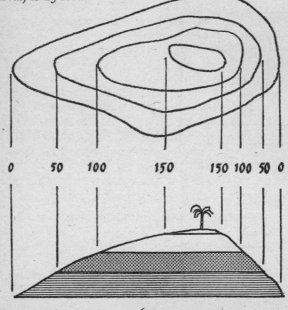

At all points along a contour line the height above sea level is the same. If you could follow a contour line, you would remain at the same level, but if you changed direction at right angles and made for the next line, the degree of slope would depend on the space between the two lines, taking into account the horizontal scale of the map.

For example, on the 1-inch O.S. map, two contour lines an inch apart would tell you that the slope of the ground was 50 feet in 1 mile, or 1,760 yards. If the lines were a tenth of an inch apart, the slope would then be 50 feet in 176 yards – ten times as steep. So, the closer together the contour lines, the steeper the slope. A glance at Dead-eye's island, around which the sea level has dropped at 50-foot intervals and left tide marks, may make this clearer.

Conventional Signs

These are map symbols. They take up less map space than a picture, or outline, or a written description, and are used on the smaller scale maps so that the maximum amount of information can be included. They are easy to learn because most of them explain themselves. Each map has a key to its symbols. O.S. conventional signs are not the same on all maps. They vary with type of map and scale. It takes years to revise a map series completely, and sometimes a new symbol is added, or an old one changed, after some of the earlier sheets have already been printed. It is wise, therefore, to check with the key before setting out with an unfamiliar map, because you depend on conventional signs for pin-pointing landmarks as well as for giving information about a place.

Here are a few details to add to what the 1-inch O.S. map key tells you:

METALLED (*road*): Metalling is broken stone used in road surfacing.

PECKED (*line*): A line broken into dots …… to indicate an unfenced road, wood, etc.

FENCED (*roads, woods, etc.*): This includes fencing as normally understood, and walls, railings, hedges, etc.

BRIDLE (*path*): Means the path can be used by horse-riders as well as walkers, and should have gates as well as stiles.

ROUGH PASTURE: This is uncultivated land, covered with bracken, heather, gorse, wild grass, or the like.

WOODS: The tree symbols are placed conventionally, simply to indicate woodland, not the positions of the trees.

PYLONS: In the Electricity Transmission Line symbol, the arrow heads representing the pylons are placed only conventionally, not where they actually stand. In a bend, where a line changes direction there will obviously be a pylon.

P (*Post Office*): This is also placed conventionally where there happens to be room for it on the map. It shows that the village has a post office, but not where it is situated.

TELEPHONE CALL BOXES (T, A, R.): These are usually in isolated roadside positions and can therefore be accurately placed on the map. They are the small black square nearest the letter T, A, or R.

L.W.M., H.W.M.: These stand for low-water mark and high-water mark respectively. The area between the two is called the foreshore.

SPOT HEIGHT: This is a height above sea level measured to the nearest foot. It is shown by a dot with a number beside it. They are often to be found marking heights along a road, and where they appear at frequent intervals they give a clear idea of the amount and direction of slope.

TRIGONOMETRICAL POINT: This is a triangulation station used by surveyors map making, and is usually marked as such at its location.

BOUNDARIES: Beware of confusing boundaries with footpaths. You are not likely to do this when out with a map, especially when the boundary runs across a lake or down the middle of a river, but it is easy enough to do indoors, planning a route. The county boundary is the one to watch. Its dashes are slightly longer than those of the footpath. When in doubt, follow it until it joins or crosses footpaths you can compare it with.

Setting your map

As we already know, a map is set, or orientated, when it is placed so that it corresponds with the ground. North on the map then points towards north on the ground. The map is then 'in gear' and ready to take you on your way. There are two methods of setting a map – by landmarks, and by knowing where north is.

To set by landmark when you know your position on the map (outside a country railway station, or at a crossroads, for example) find a landmark that you can identify on the map, turn

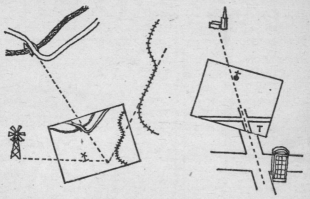

Setting a map by landmark

the map until the two positions on it are in direct line with you and the landmark, and the map is set. It can also be set by turning it to 'fit' an irregular-shaped crossroads or a T-junction, and in many other similar ways.

When you have only a rough idea of your position, such as when emerging out of a wood, you can set the map by turning it in the direction of a landmark (better still, two) identified on the map, or you can align a straight stretch of road, canal, river, or railway line on the map with the same feature on the ground. When you have no idea of your position, you need at least two identifiable landmarks.

Setting a map by knowing the direction of north is the easiest and quickest method. Ways of finding true north without a compass are explained on pages 72–9. Once you know true north, you simply turn the north point of your map towards it and it is set.

o.s. maps, and most others, are so printed that the north is at the top. Its vertical sides and grid lines therefore point

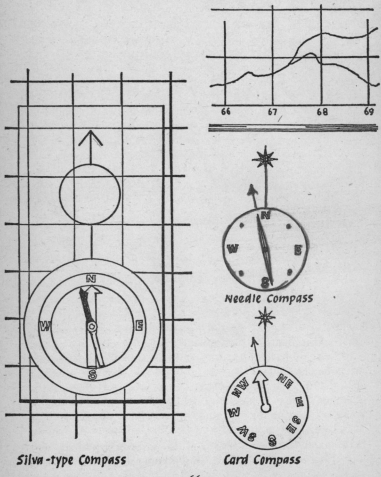

Silva-type Compass

Needle Compass

Card Compass

north and south, and its horizontal sides and grid lines point east and west. An advantage of this is that no matter how the map is folded when in use, the grid lines will always tell you where north is without having to refer to the north point in the margin.

North is shown in three ways on 1-inch O.S. maps – true, magnetic, and grid. True north corresponds to north on the ground (the direction of the north pole); magnetic north is the north indicated by a magnetic compass and is used as an aid to finding true north.

Grid north is the north indicated by the vertical grid lines on O.S. maps. Only one of these lines, the central one of the system, runs true north. That is because the grid (called the National Grid) is flat, and the earth's surface, on to which it is projected, is curved. The difference, which varies with distance from the central line, is stated at the foot of each sheet, but is so slight that it can be ignored by the general map user.

To set a map by compass, place it flat on the map with its N. and S. points in line with the map's true north and south, turn the map until the compass needle is the required number of degrees west of north, and the map is set. If the map has true and magnetic north direction arrows, as on the 1-inch map, place the compass over them with the true north aligned, then turn the map until the compass needle is over the map's magnetic north arrow.

Finding Your Position on a Map

As we have already seen, you can set a map without knowing exactly where you are, but once set, there is a good chance that you will eventually find out. Eventually finding out can waste time and energy, so it is better if you can find your position without having to go any farther than is necessary to spot landmarks or ground features that you can also locate on your map. From such a vantage point you can find your position with or without a compass.

With a compass: Take bearings on two (or three) landmarks and plot them on the map. The point where the bearings cross is

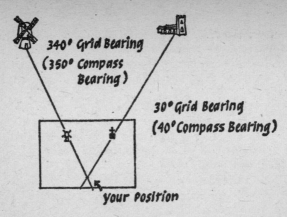

340° Grid Bearing
(350° Compass
Bearing)

30° Grid Bearing
(40° Compass Bearing)

your position

Finding your position by compass

your position. Plot (draw) the lines lightly with a pencil, or use straight-edged paper, or simply your imagination. The Silva-type compass makes plotting easy and accurate.

Without a compass: In one direction find two landmarks or features which are in direct line with you. In another direction find two more in direct line. Plot or imagine these lines on the map. The point where they cross is your position. You will almost certainly have to change your position to bring yourself into direct line with the selected objects. Use anything at all that can be identified on the map, such as the corner of a wood, a bridge, road junction, or a bend in a road, river, or railway.

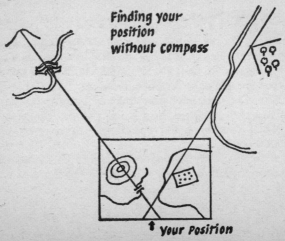

Finding your
position
without compass

your position

Map References

The grid of lines which Dead-eye drew on his map, and the numbering of each line, as well as the further dividing of the sides of each square into imaginary thirds, enabled him and any holder of a copy of the map to locate or refer to any part of the island.

The grid on your 1-inch O.S. map is similar, but the sides of each square are divided into imaginary tenths, and as each side is 1 kilometre long – about 1,100 yards, it means that you can give a reference that pin-points a place to the nearest 110 yards. This would have to be a six-figure reference – two figures for each line, eastward and northward; and one figure each for the tenths, eastward and northward. The tenths are quite easily estimated by eye, but a gadget called a 'romer' can be used for greater accuracy.

The map reference system now used on all Ordnance Survey maps is based on a system of vertical and horizontal lines known as the National Grid, and covers the whole of Britain.

When it is necessary to show that a group of figures is a map reference or grid reference (both the same thing), it is prefixed by M.R. or G.R., e.g. M.R.123456 or G.R.123456.

6. Figure Grid Reference

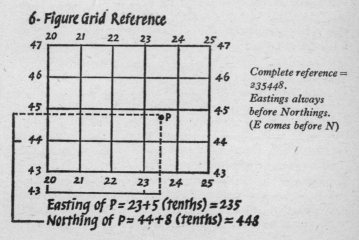

Complete reference = 235448.
Eastings always before Northings.
(E comes before N)

Easting of P = 23 + 5 (tenths) = 235
Northing of P = 44 + 8 (tenths) = 448

Reading a Map

One way to become an efficient map reader is to start off with a 1-inch O.S. map in an area you already know, and without being concerned about getting anywhere in particular take a leisurely look at the way the various features of the area are represented on the map.

Take an extra look at anything that might have misled you had you been a stranger, such as the T-junction that looks like a fork; or the crossroads that is really a T-junction with another road some yards away, and which is clear enough when you take a closer look at the map; or the little bend in the road which cannot be shown because of the small scale of the map. Compare everything in sight – road slope with contour lines or spot heights; distances long and short between identifiable points; all conventional signs, and the rest – and at the end of it you can be sure you will already be a better map reader than you were when you started out.

Before setting out with an unfamiliar map, check the scale and the vertical interval of contours. And look the conventional signs over, because there are some variations on O.S. maps of different series.

When you set out, try to visualize from the map the country between you and your destination. Picture in your mind, if you can, the route beyond your present view – what is round the corner or over the hill. With this general picture in your mind, and some idea of the mileage to cover and the time it should take you, you will be much less likely to lose your way.

Conventional signs help you to check your position and to keep to your planned route. When there are none where you need them, use other means, such as the corner of a wood, a bend in a river or road. A wide sweeping curve in a road or path has a different compass direction at all points, so use your compass to tell you where you are.

When you leave a road for a footpath, check with your compass your general direction in case it peters out (possibly ploughed over) or branches into several unmapped paths. Look ahead for stiles. Find a landmark in the direction you want to go, then you can take your eyes off the compass.

Contours can help you when in doubt, by telling you whether you should be climbing, descending or keeping level, especially when a path branches unexpectedly (and unmapped) or when travelling through dense woodland.

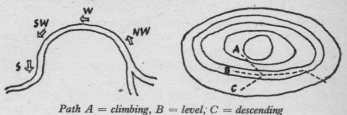

Path A = climbing, B = level, C = descending

Planning a Route

Two important factors when planning a route are distance and time. Whether the route covers a day's duration or a fortnight's, the planning is based on time. First you decide on the duration, say, a weekend. Next comes walking speed (a cyclist would do 30 to 40 miles a day on holiday, but more normally). In moderate country and with a 20-lb pack, you will average about $2\frac{1}{2}$ miles an hour.

From your intended arrival time at the camp site you now work backwards to your midday mealtime, allow time for a meal and a rest, then work back to your start time.

As for the route itself, you will plan your midday stop according to your starting time and estimated walking speed. You will keep an eye on contours, remembering that paths which follow contour lines give you level walking, and that the nearer to right angles to them you walk the steeper it will be. Remember also, when measuring distance on your map, that 1 inch equals 1 mile in flat country only; in undulating country that same inch on the map can be much more than a mile on the ground. When it is not easy to tell from contours which way the ground slopes, look for the nearest stream and recall that water flows downhill. You will, of course, choose a route that makes the hike worth the effort.

WITHOUT A COMPASS

THE wise hiker in strange country always carries a compass, but things go wrong sometimes and compasses get damaged, or lost or left behind.

In such a case of need, it helps if you can manage without a compass by making use of any natural or man-made direction pointers that may be present.

The natural pointers are the sun, the moon and stars, and nature's clues known to backwoodsmen as 'sign'. Man-made clues do not need the keen and practised eye that is required to 'read' natural sign reliably, but they are not so likely to be found off the beaten track, which is usually where you are when you get lost.

Direction finding is primarily a matter of finding north, and from it any other compass point. The following methods are only makeshift substitutes, but they can be very welcome at times. They range from good to poor, but tend to become more reliable with practice and experience.

THE SUN

First, let us look at the sun's daily journey across the sky. We know, of course, that the sun's apparent clockwise movement is due to the earth's counter-clockwise rotation. Generally speaking, the sun rises in the east, climbs higher until it is due south, then begins sinking towards the west, where it sets. Out of sight (during the night), the sun continues sinking until it is due north, then starts rising towards the east, where it appears again to begin a new day. During the long summer days the sun rises earlier (north of east) and sets later (north of west), and during the short winter days it rises later (south of east) and sets earlier (south of west).

Because of the earth's non-circular orbit and the sun's one-sided position in it, the sun is a fairly inaccurate direction pointer, except at noon (G.M.T.) when it is at its highest point in the sky and always within 4° of south. Therefore, when shadows are at their shortest they are pointing north.

The sun's timetable (G.M.T.) is approximately as follows:

6 a.m.	Due east	Shadows long and pointing west
9 a.m.	Due south-east	Shadows shortening and pointing north-west
12 noon	Due south	Shadows at shortest and pointing north
3 p.m.	Due south-west	Shadows lengthening and pointing north-east
6 p.m.	Due west	Shadows long and pointing east

You will see from the timetable how the sun's position can be used as a rough guide to direction. Rough, because the sun can be an hour (15°) slow on a summer morning and an hour fast the same afternoon. Even so, direction reliable only to the nearest 20° can sometimes be better than no idea of direction at all, especially over short distances. Here are some ways of using the sun.

TIME OF DAY

By knowing the time of day, the sun's approximate compass direction can be found. In reverse, knowing the sun's position by compass will give you some idea of the time.

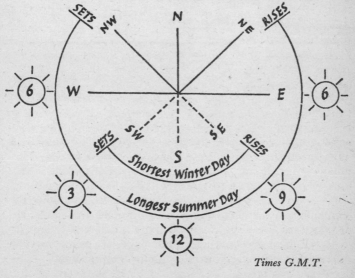

Times G.M.T.

BY WATCH

The sun-and-watch method gives a more accurate result. The watch is held flat, with the hour hand pointing at the sun. It can be positioned correctly by holding a pin or matchstick upright over the end of the hour hand and turning the watch until the shadow is over the centre of the face. Now the angle the hour hand makes with the figure 12 (figure 1 where clock time is an hour ahead) is bisected (halved) giving a north–south line. The reason for bisecting is that the hour hand travels at twice the speed of the sun. If it travelled at the same speed, the figure 12 (or 1) would point south whenever the hour hand was turned towards the sun – if, of course, the sun was as good a timekeeper as the watch.

Sun and Watch Method

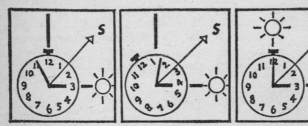

Greenwich Mean Time: A line midway between 12 and the hour hand gives south (approx)

British Summer Time: A line midway between 1 and the hour hand gives south (approx)

Southern Hemisphere: A line midway between 12 and the hour hand gives north (approx)

BY SHADOW

This method can be resorted to when you have no watch and no idea of the time. It can give only general direction. The most it can tell you, unless the sun is near the south, is the quarter of the compass (the quadrant) the sun happens to be in. This is arrived at by noting the sun's movement, either by checking it in relation to objects on the ground (trees, hills), or by shadows. If the sun is still climbing (shadows shortening), it is in the east–south quadrant; if it has begun to sink (shadows lengthening) it is in the south–west quadrant.

NATURAL SIGN

Most of nature's clues to direction are due to the sun keeping itself to roughly one half of our sky. It is never in the north, so exposed objects have a sunny side and a side that is always in the shade, and likely to be damp. Where these opposite conditions show a difference you have a clue to direction. For example, moss is found on the north side of trees, boulders, and the like, because it thrives in damp conditions. Tree bark is often lighter in colour on the drier (south) side. It is also thinner on the south side of most trees, causing the heart to be towards the south, as can been seen on tree stumps. Sunlight also affects the growth of branches and leaves.

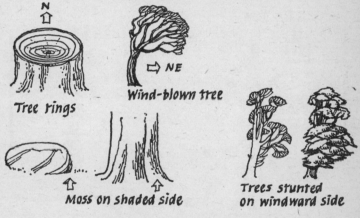

N

Tree rings

⇨ NE

Wind-blown tree

Moss on shaded side

Trees stunted on windward side

Our prevailing south-west wind makes its mark too. It can incline trees towards the north-east by its continual pressure, and it can stunt a tree's growth on the windward side.

A backwoodsman using natural sign to find his way would never depend on any single observation. He would take several and crosscheck. To be able to read natural sign reliably requires practice. It is almost useless to try your skill for the first time when you are actually lost. It is much better to see what clues you can find in an area you know, and check each with a compass. Reasoning out why sometimes a clue gives a wrong direction is the best way to become efficient – the east side of a tree being mossier, for instance, due to the shape of the trunk channelling excess rain to that side; or rocks or buildings deflecting the prevailing wind.

Even the village street with its sunblinds along one side only, is a direction clue.

THE MOON

When the moon is full it is directly opposite the sun, so its journey across the night sky is a repeat of the sun's day journey, but twelve hours later. A full moon, therefore, can be used for direction finding in all the ways already suggested for the sun. The moon is also useful at other phases, as shown.

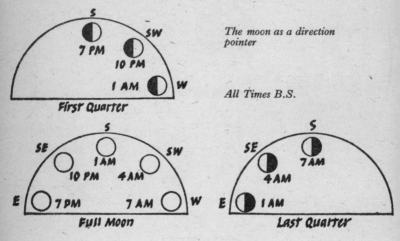

The moon as a direction pointer

All Times B.S.

First Quarter

Full Moon

Last Quarter

THE STARS

The Pole Star is the most accurate of all direction pointers. It is at the centre (almost) of the revolving pattern of stars, revolving in its own small circle about 2° across, and so never more than 1° off true north. It is always at the same height (altitude) above the horizon as the observer's latitude, so in London its altitude is $51\frac{1}{2}°$, and in Edinburgh it is 56°. There are many ways of finding the Pole Star, as shown here.

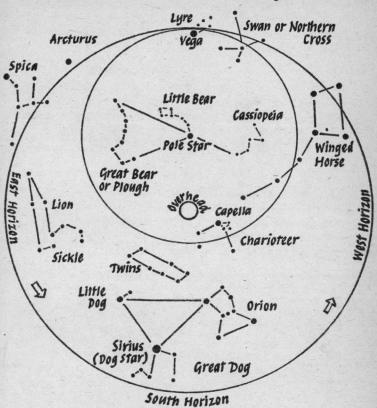

NIGHT SKY

As seen at midnight on New Year's Eve.

Eagle

Lyre

Swan or Northern Cross

Vega

Arcturus

Spica

Little Bear

Cassiopeia

Pole Star

Winged Horse

Great Bear or Plough

Overhead

Capella

East Horizon

West Horizon

Lion

Charioteer

Sickle

Twins

Little Dog

Orion

Sirius (Dog Star)

Great Dog

South Horizon

Six hours earlier, the Winged Horse (now setting in the north-west) was where Orion now is, and Orion was rising in the east.

The stars in the smaller circle are called circumpolar stars because, unlike those outside it, they never set and can be seen all the year round.

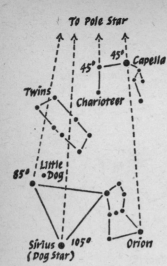

Autumn–Winter stars

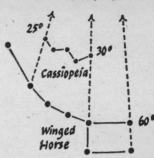

Summer–Autumn–Winter stars

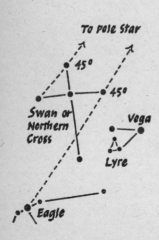

*Late Spring–Summer–
Autumn stars*

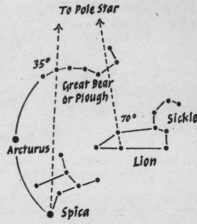

Winter–Spring stars

78

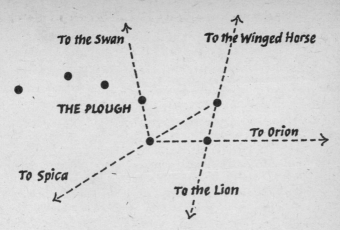

Guide to the North-Pointer Star-Groups

MAN-MADE CLUES

These are generally in places where you could just as easily ask the way, but some can be helpful at a distance. The country church is one of these. Nine out of ten are aligned east to west, and if the tower or spire is not in the middle it is at the west end. If there is more than one roof level, the lower is at the east end. Other clues are shown here.

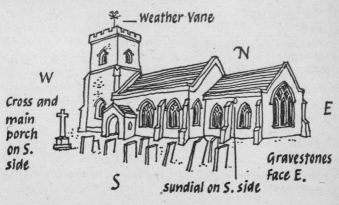

When you get there

PITCHING CAMP

CAMP sites are of many kinds, and can be grouped in different ways. There are large and small commercially run sites where everything is laid on, and where campcraft is hardly needed. There are sites run by organizations – the Scout Movement, the Camping Club, and others – where much is laid on, and where the campcraft experts are to be found, but where the beginner can get along quite happily. And there are the casual sites, such as the corner of a field offered by a farmer to an unexpected caller, or a field rented to a Scout Troop for its annual camp.

It is the casual site which calls for campcraft. Here are to be found the real joys of camping – or the miseries, depending on how you go about it.

Campcraft quickly becomes second nature to the keen new camper. He finds himself doing the right thing almost without thinking, especially after he has done it wrong once or twice. He soon discovers also, on meeting other campers, that there is often more than one right way of doing a thing. He makes his own choice. There are no hard and fast rules. He builds up his own mental rule book as he goes along. If he pitches his tent where it fills with smoke from his fire, he grumbles, moves one or the other, and makes himself a rule about noting wind direction in future. When he hears of a camper who woke up in a pool of water one night because the edge of his ground-sheet was protruding outside the tent and collecting rain off the walls, he makes sure it will never happen to him.

The casual-site camper first finds his site, decides how to make the best use of it, then sets up his camp.

Choosing a Site

The hike-camper in search of a site should allow himself ample time to find one, settle in, and make a hot drink or a meal before dark. Permission should always be sought before pitching a tent or lighting a fire.

Standing-camps are planned in advance, and the selection of the site calls for some care. Much of what is looked for applies also to hike sites, but the hike-camper can seldom be so fussy and often has to depend on his campcraft to manage with what he gets.

The experienced camper looking for a site for a standing-camp would hope to find one that is fairly open and gets sunshine, has a pleasant view and is sheltered from the prevailing wind – the usual wind direction in that place. The wind blows from the south-west three days out of four in most places in the British Isles.

The soil is important. He would avoid clay because it is brick-hard when dry, gluey when wet, and always drains badly. Stony ground makes pegging difficult, and light sandy soil does not grip pegs well. Most other soils are suitable.

Hollows are to be avoided because they are likely to be marshy after rain. Thick, lush grass usually indicates water-holding ground and, as well as being popular with midges, it stays wet too long after rain or heavy dew. Short springy grass means dry ground. A gentle slope, slightly higher than the surrounding ground, and sheltered by trees, hedge, or wall, makes a good tent site.

Water and wood (if cooking on a fire) and food supplies are essentials. He would want pure water and ample suitable wood fairly near, and the village not too distant.

The site would not have to be overlooked by houses or the public, or shared with farm animals, especially if there are lightweight tents. The distance of the nearest public transport might also have to be considered.

If, after seeing or imagining the site in the worst weather conditions, he decided it was suitable, he would next find out what supplies could be got from the farm and locally (delivered or to fetch), and the location of the nearest doctor, telephone, and post office.

The regular camper soon develops an eye for a site, and can usually tell at a glance what is worth a second look, and what is not.

Site Layout

Having got our site, we now want to make the best use of it. We camp for pleasure, so we should make our camp as comfortable a place to live in as we know how.

Wind direction, more than anything else, decides for us where best to locate the different parts of a camp, whether it is a one-tent hike-camp, a weekend Scout Patrol camp or a standing-camp. Their relative positions to leeward (following the direction of the wind) should be – living tents, store tents (in shade, facing sunless north), kitchen, washplace, latrine.

Living tents should be in the open, in a sheltered position, with their backs to the prevailing wind; not under trees, because of dripping water during (and long after) rain, and the danger of falling branches. Elms are particularly dangerous.

The tents should be on fairly level ground with a rain-draining slope gentle enough to sleep on. Haystacks and buildings are not the best places to pitch your tent in the lee of – eddying winds play odd tricks – a wall or hedge is much better.

Morning sun on tents, to dry them out after a night's rain or dew, is better than afternoon sun. A shaded tent at the hottest time of day is always welcome. It is better for the tent, too.

The kitchen should be away from the living tents, and grouped with the store tent, chopping area, and dining shelter (if any), and should if possible be nearest the wood and water supply.

The washplace and latrines should be out of view from the camp centre and, if possible, not more than 100 yards away.

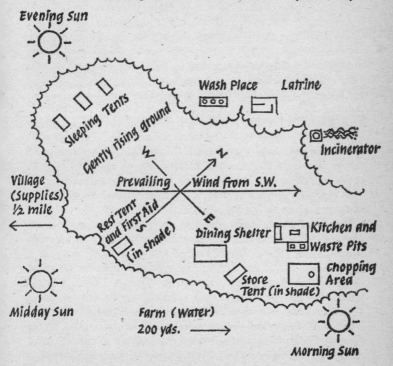

Pitching a Tent

The method of pitching a tent varies according to type, and there are often different ways of pitching the same tent. The best way is the one you find easiest and quickest. It is always advisable to practise your pitching in private before going out with a new or unfamiliar tent. Three or four trial pitchings and you will feel like an old-timer. Let us suppose you have a new lightweight ridge tent with walls.

Take the tent out of its bag. Note carefully how it is folded. Spread it out with the door facing the desired direction and with the four corners roughly where they are to be when pitched.

Start by pegging the door flaps down where the front pole will be. Square the front of the tent exactly where you want it to face, and peg the two corners down. Now square off and peg the back corners down. Next, put in the back and front main-guy pegs at nearly the tent's length away, hook the guys on and adjust slightly slack.

Unpeg the door flaps and put the front and back poles in position. They will stay put while you correctly adjust the main guys. Lastly, peg out the side guys and put the rest of the wall pegs in. Make any necessary adjustments. Poles should stand straight; side guys should be in line with seams and follow the same slope as the roof; and pegs should be at an angle of 45°.

If the pegs form a geometrical pattern round the tent, and the guys are equally tensioned, it will stand trim and without sag or crease. In windy weather, start by pegging the back corners down so that the canvas will be blowing away from you.

Wall-less ridge tent: Pitch as for ridge tent with walls, except for the side guys.

Lightweight with ridge pole: Peg down two side corners. Slip the assembled ridge and upright poles into the tent. With front and back main guys in one hand, pull the tent upright and hook a centre side guy over a peg already in place. A peg or two at the pole butts will prevent them slipping while raising

84

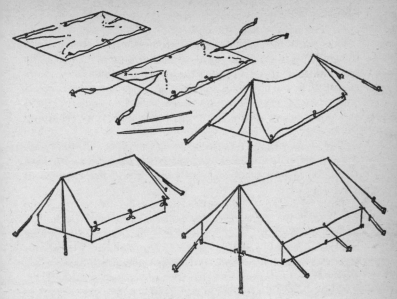

Pitching a light-weight ridge single handed

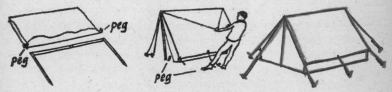

peg

peg

peg

Pitching a small ridge tent single handed

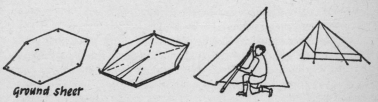

Ground sheet

Pitching a one-pole tent

the poles. Peg down the remaining two corners. Correct the poles. Peg main guys, side guys, and the rest of the walls.

One-pole tent: Place its shaped groundsheet where you want the tent. Peg the walls down all round (or bottom edge, if wall-less). Raise it upright by its pole. Peg guys down. The tent's centre back, butt of pole, and main guy peg should be in line.

Tents with sewn-in groundsheets are the easiest to pitch. Peg groundsheet down. Position pole or poles. Peg according to type.

The smaller frame tents are also easy to pitch once the frame is assembled. Fitting the cover in a wind, work with your back to the wind (the windward side) and it will help instead of hindering.

Full-sized ridge-poled tents require at least three people to pitch. Start by laying the ridge pole on the ground in the line of pitching. Knock a wall peg in at each end as a guide to where the uprights are to stand. Now, lay the tent flat. Fit the uprights into the ridge pole and push them carefully into the tent and up to the ridge so that the pole spikes go through the grommet holes. Place the main guys (if separate) on the spikes. The tent is now raised, and held upright while the main guys are pegged down. Then, all hands to the pegging.

Fly-sheets are easiest fitted after the tent is erected. Throw the fly-sheet over the tent, place the separators on the pole spikes, then the fly-sheet grommet holes on the spikes, and peg the guys down. In a wind, peg one side down before throwing over. In a gale, roll the fly-sheet up, peg one side down, then roll it over the tent and secure it on the other side to pegs already placed. There should be complete clearance between a fly-sheet and its tent.

When main guys are crossed backwards (stormset) to prevent billowing, there should be clearance between them and the canvas, and between the guys themselves, to reduce chafing.

Lay the groundsheet so that that it covers the mud-walling all the way round to keep draughts out, but first remove any stones and anything else that could break through when trodden on.

Bivouac or Hike-sheet

The bivouac shelter is the simplest form of tent, as well as the lightest and cheapest, and can be put to dozens of other uses. It is merely a sheet of proofed cloth, 7 to 10 feet square; with eyelets, or D-rings on tapes, about 18 inches apart along each side.

Cloth: Any strong, closely woven fabric such as cotton cambric. Nylon, terylene, lightweight plastic-coated groundsheet cloth, and similar fabrics normally unsuitable for tents because of condensation, make good hike-sheets. The weight should be about 3 oz per square yard. The commonest cloth widths are 36, 42, 48, and 54 inches. Nine yards of 36- or 42-inch cloth cut into three and sewn together, or four yards of 48- or 56-inch cloth cut in half and sewn together, would make a suitable size of sheet.

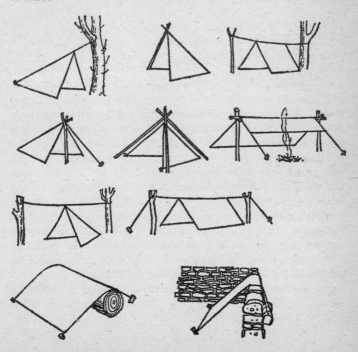

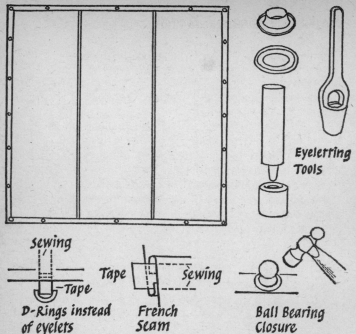

Eyeletting Tools

sewing

Tape

Tape

D-Rings instead of eyelets

Sewing

French Seam

Ball Bearing Closure

Making: The sewing is best done on an electric sewing machine, using a fine needle and strong cotton. A french seam, with ½-inch-wide linen tape inserted and sewn through, makes a good reinforced job of it. If there is a ridge seam, the tape can be extended a few inches beyond the edge, then folded back and sewn down with a D-ring enclosed.

Eyeletting: Eyelets and eyeletting tools can be bought from most tent suppliers. If you cut the holes instead of using a punch, make them a close fit. A ball-bearing and a hammer can be used for splaying the closure over the washer. Make sure the cloth is firmly held all the way round. An eyelet with a ½-inch diameter hole is about right. 8-oz cord or similar light line is suitable for guys, with or without runners.

Proofing: Silicone-based proofing solutions are very effective on lightweight fabrics. They can be bought at Scout Shops and other camp equipment suppliers.

With Lashings   **Without Lashings**

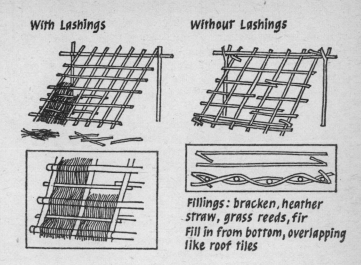

Fillings: bracken, heather
straw, grass reeds, fir
Fill in from bottom, overlapping
like roof tiles

Latrine and Washplace

The latrine should be one of the first parts of camp to be set up. Ideally, it will be 50 to 100 yards to leeward (downwind) of the living tents, screened with hessian or canvas about 6 feet high, and hidden from view by natural cover. If it is below the level of the rest of the site, where there are no nearby water supplies to percolate into, so much the better. Clay soil drains very slowly and should be avoided, if possible.

A latrine trench about 3 feet long, 1 foot wide, and 2 feet deep (6 inches deeper in clay), is sufficient for ten boys for two days, after which it is filled in and a new one dug. The loose earth (kept dry, if possible) is piled behind the trench and a trowel or something similar provided for scattering in coverage after use. Complete coverage is very important. Disinfectant then becomes unnecessary and flies stay away whose next call might well have been the camp kitchen. Paper is kept under a waterproof cover or in a box with lid. A shallow pit lined with stones, and screened off, serves as a urinal.

There should be a washbasin and towel outside the latrine. At night, a lamp should be placed where it can be seen from the tents, for taking into the latrine, and later replacing.

Lightweight campers will use natural or improvised screening. A hole should not be dug in a place which might be selected as a tent site by a following camper, such as the shelter of a hedge or wall.

Washplaces should be sited similarly to latrines, chiefly for the reasons of the seeping away of dirty water. A soakage pit 9 to 12 inches square and deep (or according to need, and type of soil) should be dug a few yards away and covered in the same way as a wet pit, and the trapped soap waste periodically buried or burned. The soakage pit prevents the area becoming a marsh.

Before using a stream for washing make sure that it is not being polluted upstream, and that you would not be polluting it for animals or others downstream.

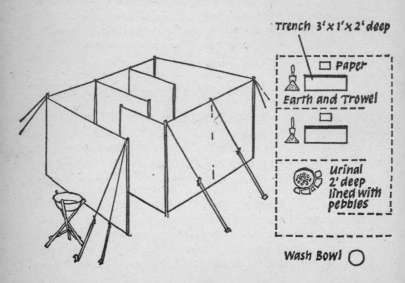

Trench 3' x 1' x 2' deep

☐ Paper

Earth and Trowel

Urinal 2' deep lined with pebbles

Wash Bowl ◯

Camp Routine

A routine is an orderly way of doing something. Often without realizing it the good camper has his own pet routine for almost everything he does. He learned early in his camping life that the opposite of routine is muddle, and that muddle wastes time and energy, and can take all the pleasure out of camping. When he packs his rucksack he knows at once what goes in next, and so he knows exactly where everything is. His tent-pitching routine becomes so automatic that he can pitch his tent in total darkness. When he lights his cooking fire he already has enough fuel for the job on hand and the cooking pots are ready to go on. And when he has finished his meal there is hot water ready for the washing up. The inside of his tent is without muddle too, and what is not stowed in his rucksack is kept neatly together. Anything he needs he can lay his hand on at once, even in the dark.

A lone camper or a small group of campers can vary their daily routine to suit themselves, or have none at all if they are not real campers, but a large standing-camp, such as a Scout Troop's annual camp, must have a daily routine. It must be known to all the campers and they must abide by it. Here is a typical Scout camp daily routine:

7.00	Campers roused. Wash, etc.
8.15	Breakfast
8.45	Washing up. Cleaning tents and ground. Airing bedding
10.00	Inspection. Flag break. Prayers
10.15	Scouting activities
1.00	Dinner
1.30	Quiet hour (Resting, reading, writing)
2.30	Wide games and Scout activities
5.00	Tea
6.00	Camp games or free time
8.00	Light supper
8.30	Camp fire
9.30	Prayers
10.00	Lights out. Silence after 10.30

No matter how small your camp, if you base it on a simple routine it will be a smoother-running camp, and therefore a happier one. Here are some points to bear in mind:

Sleeping: A good night's sleep is important, especially to the hike-camper, so if there is more than one sleeping tent, agree times between which there will be silence in camp, say, between 10.30 p.m. and 7.00 a.m.

Bedding: Sleeping bags, blankets, and nightwear absorb moisture from the body during the night and, unless they are dried out (aired) in the open each day, will eventually become damp enough to keep you awake at night with cold. So, get them outside in the morning sunshine, spread out for an hour or two over a hedge (not still wet with dew), fence, line, or piece of gadgetry, but preferably not over your tent.

The tent: Air the tent too – and the ground it stands on, to keep it sweet. Get everything outside on a groundsheet. Brail (tie up) the tent walls. If the tent has no walls, unpeg the sunny or windy side and throw it right over. Tents with sewn-in groundsheets should be brushed out. A clothes-line in a tent is not a good idea: it restricts valuable headroom.

Eating: Aim at fixed mealtimes, all eating together rather than at staggered and haphazard times to suit individual whims and fancies. Wash up as soon as the meal is over. It makes the job easier. The site will look better for it too, especially if you rig up a few gadgets that keep things off the ground and together, either all in one place or beside each tent.

Before turning in: If using a wood fire, douse it and see that you have dry wood for the morning, unless it can be left smouldering overnight under a cover or a log without danger from flying sparks in the event of a wind getting up. Cover wood and water supplies, and see that nothing is left outside that is better kept dry, such as the axe or clothing. Check that all pegs are firm, and slacken all guys slightly because dew (heaviest on still, clear evenings) shrinks guys and canvas. No naked lights in tents. If using a candle, see that it is contained in a candle lantern.

Health in Camp

Camping out and being fit and healthy mean one and the same thing to most campers. Even so, campers do catch colds and chills and other minor ailments, though the victims are more likely to be new campers learning by the hard way. More serious can be the effects of bad water (which usually looks good) and food contaminated by flies.

Water: At worst, drinking bad water can give you typhoid and kill you; at best, it can mildly upset your stomach. So take care. Always inquire locally about water fit for drinking. Streams or springs above the level of human habitation are generally safe to drink, but below it they could be polluted by household outflow. Whenever in doubt, boil water for about five minutes. Water purifying tablets can be bought at chemists' shops.

Food poisoning: This is uncommon in camp, but when it does occur it is likely to result from bad hygiene (mostly poor latrine drill, unwashed hands, and faulty grease traps), which is also bad camping. Flies, with their six sticky feet, will be attracted to the latrine if there is not sufficient coverage after use. Food not properly covered in the store tent, hanging larder, or elsewhere; or food in the kitchen or on your plate; may next receive the same six sticky, germ-laden feet. Decaying food that has slipped through the grease-pit cover becomes, like an ill-kept latrine, a breeding ground for flies. The eggs are laid in the decaying matter, and after the quickly hatched-out maggots have grown fat on it they become pupae, which in turn become a new batch of flies. And so the breeding goes on as long as breeding places are provided for them.

Mild cases of food poisoning right themselves in a few days, but serious ones need a doctor.

Sleep: A good night's sleep is essential to good health. Avoid sleeping in anything you have worn (especially next to your skin) during the day. Keep warm in dry nightwear and bedding. Have tent doors open if weather permits. Don't put your day clothes in a closed-up polythene bag: give the day's body moisture a chance to evaporate out. Air your bedding daily, as well as tent and tent space, and dry out anything that needs it.

Personal hygiene: Have an all-over wash daily if possible, or cover the whole area in instalments of a half or a third at a time. Give your teeth and feet regular daily attention. The inner workings are sometimes affected by change of water, food, and activity, in which case seek mild aid from the medicine box.

Camp wear: Sandals or plimsolls and no stockings, are best in dewy grass or rain. Bare feet is not a good idea, except for finding sharp stones and broken glass. Shorts and open-necked shirt are the best upper wear.

Sun: Too much sun too soon can ruin camp for you, and give you long and painful days and nights. Break yourself in gradually. In hot weather, keep in the shade between eleven and four o'clock, or wear light clothing with long sleeves. If you are fair or red-haired, take extra care. Calamine lotion or bicarbonate of soda solution relieves sunburning.

Rain: If you get wet through, strip off, have a rub down, and change into dry clothes and you will be none the worse for it, especially if you follow it with a hot drink. Always carry a change of clothing, even if it is only a jersey and football shorts.

Rest: A quiet, restful hour after the midday meal is good for your stomach, and for you in general. A useful item of kit is a piece of plastic or other waterproof cloth, about 15 inches square, for sitting on instead of on the ground, which is nearly always damp. Better still, make a bag of it by sewing a piece of cotton or woollen cloth to it, and stuffing it with spare clothing to make a cushion or pillow of it.

The Countryside at Night

New campers sometimes find night-time in camp strange and rather alarming. The distant hoot of an owl, the churring of a nightjar, the bark of a fox, and the whining of the wind, are as much a part of camp to the seasoned camper as the smell of woodsmoke is. Without its night sounds and shadows, camp would lose much of its enchantment. Night creatures no doubt have their own ideas about campers and other day creatures.

The shadowy tree which seems to point menacing fingers at you by night, is the same friendly tree you saw earlier in the day, and will see again tomorrow. The two greeny-blue eyes staring at you from the hedge are only a pair of lady glow-worms. The dozens of pairs of yellow eyes your torch picks out over the camp hedge are sheep looking your way. The foot-steps around your tent which you keep getting out of bed to

investigate are a horse clomping about in the next field, or even two fields away.

There is much less to get alarmed about in the country at night than in the town at night.

Sleep Well

One of the commonest reasons for the once-only camper crying 'Never again!' is sleepless nights in a chilly bed.

A groundsheet keeps only the damp out, not the cold. The only way to be warm in blankets (no fewer than two, and all-wool) is to have at least as many layers under you as over you. The fluffiness of the dry wool acts as an insulator and prevents the heat of your body flowing away into the ground, in the same way that electricity will not pass through a porcelain insulator.

There are various ways of making up a bed which give you several thicknesses above and below. You can further insulate yourself, if necessary, by putting a layer of spare clothing underneath you. Still more effective are newspapers or brown paper. The wearing of socks and sweater help on a really cold night.

Sleeping bags with simple quilting, unlike box or wall quilting, insulate only where the filling is, and not along the rows of stitching forming the compartments which keep the filling evenly distributed throughout the bag. Suitable insulation for this type of bag is a ground blanket strip – any piece of all-wool cloth about 2 feet wide and the length of the bag, or from hips to shoulders.

The best blankets or sleeping bag obtainable will not keep you warm when damp, so always keep your bedding well aired and dry.

A word of warning: a newly dry-cleaned sleeping bag should be well aired before using – the fumes can be fatal. A 'Space' blanket, or thin plastic sheeting, should not be allowed to cover the face – they can suffocate.

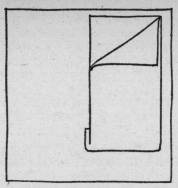

3-Pin Blanket Bed

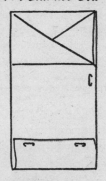

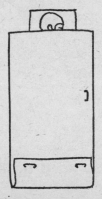

Bad Weather

Rain and wind are the two elements of weather which the camper is happiest to be without. At home in bad weather wet clothes can be dried or replaced several times a day without much bother or ill effect. In camp, with one set of dry spares at most and little chance of drying wet clothes while rain continues, keeping things dry (especially bedding) is very important.

Start by making the tent as leak-proof as possible. Rain shrinks tent fabric as well as guys. To get the best rain protection a tent or fly-sheet is capable of, especially an old one, slacken the guys almost to sagging point, and when they tighten up again (which they will) slacken again. Repeat this until there is no shrinkage left, and leave just taut. To do this with a wall-less tent known to leak, the pole or poles would have to be sunk a few inches into the ground, or the pegs (and groundsheet) brought in an inch or two.

Keep all clothes and bedding away from tent sides. Fold the groundsheet back from the door so that you can enter with wet shoes and remove them without soiling the groundsheet.

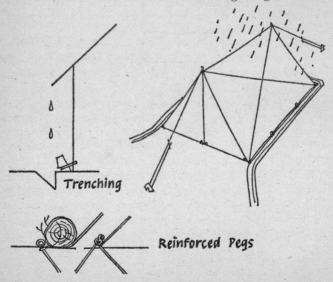

Trenching

Reinforced Pegs

Use only one door flap until the ground begins to get soggy, then peg it down and use the other for a while, or change to the opposite end if the tent is double-ended.

If rain starts running under the tent, the only alternative to moving the tent is to dig a shallow V-shaped trench to carry the water away and to lead it where it will not form a puddle. Keep the soil off the canvas. Soil rots canvas.

A tent without a fly-sheet is likely to leak wherever you touch it on the inside. The dripping can usually be stopped by running a finger down the canvas from the leak to the ground, but only lightly enough to direct the stream of water, otherwise you will have more leaks than you can cope with. Draw the groundsheet clear of the drips.

In high wind tighten all guys, and reinforce pegs if necessary. If the wind is blowing towards the tent doors, keep them shut to prevent ballooning. Storm-set guys help keep the canvas under control.

FIRES, FUEL, AND STOVES

WOOD fire or pressure stove? Some campers are scornful of fires, others are just as scornful of stoves. Some make the best use of both. Each has its points for and against.

The stove is better for the hiker out for the day, who likes to make himself a fresh, hot drink of tea or soup wherever and whenever he feels like it. And it is better for the hike-camper not knowing where he will stop next. Wood fires are not always allowed, and they are dependent on wood supplies. They also take up time wood-gathering, lighting, and tending. Another advantage to the hike-camper is that he needs hardly any more room for his camp site than his tent takes up. His pots and pans are also easier to keep clean.

The wood fire has one great advantage over the stove – it is adjustable to the needs of the moment. The little fire boiling an egg for one, can be extended to cook a three-course meal for a dozen. You can have boiling heat at one part of the fire, and simmering heat at another. The number of pots it can be made to cope with at any one time makes up for time lost in getting wood. Camp without a fire and the smell of wood smoke is, to many a camper, no camp at all, just tents in a field. Wooding, firelighting, and cooking on an open fire are, to such a camper, part of the fun and adventure of camping, and he has nothing to carry but matches.

At open-fire standing-camps it is wise to have a pressure stove in case of emergency.

Fires

In camp, fires for sing-songs, for drying clothes, for signalling, or as beacons for late-arrivals, are just fires, not much different from one another – but not so the cooking fire. There are as many kinds of cooking fire as there are shapes of tents. Some of the commoner ones are shown here. Like all the others, each is designed primarily to do the same thing in a different way – to keep a pot or pan a few inches above a fire. Some, such as the reflector fire, are designed for a special purpose.

Open-ground cross-bar, crane, and tripod fires are not very efficient because too much heat is lost to the air, and unless a bar or crane is adjustable, or you have various sizes of pothook, you can use only one size of cooking utensil.

The altar fire is popular with standing-camps and on permanent camp sites. It is a fire raised to about waist level to save back bending. At that height, the wind tends to whip sparks around. Care is needed to avoid dixies overspilling while being lifted, and to ensure they do not topple off.

Perhaps the most efficient general-purpose fire, and certainly the most popular with hike-camper and period-camper alike, is the hunter's fire. It has many variations – the trench, the lumberman's, the brick fire, are a few.

The points in favour of this type of fire are that the logs, bricks, or trench can be positioned to receive the prevailing wind; little heat is lost, especially with the trench fire; and as there is a wide end to receive the wind, and a narrow end, it can support pots and pans of different sizes, or greensticks for spit-cooking.

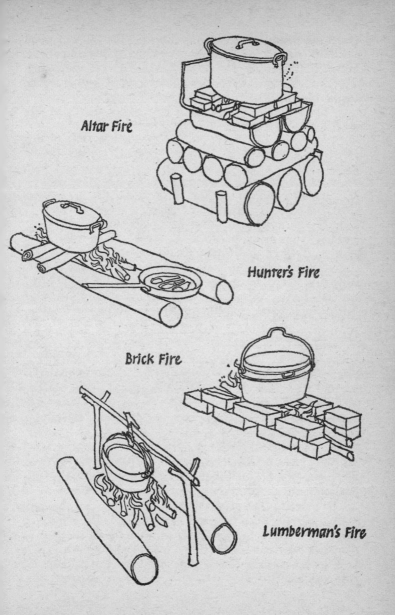

Altar Fire

Hunter's Fire

Brick Fire

Lumberman's Fire

Kinds of Wood

The new camper who does not know one wood from another will get little help from a long list telling him that this one burns well or badly, and that one spits, sparks, crackles, smokes, burns too quickly or too slowly, or not at all. There are about 1,800 species of trees and shrubs in the British Isles, and though the average camper is likely to meet only about sixty of the commoner trees, even that is plenty when most of them seem to look alike.

The easiest way to know the good woods is to learn the bad ones, because there are so few of them. Of the sixty trees, about a dozen are cone-bearing – pines, spruces, firs, cedars, larch. These are the resinous softwoods, mostly sparking, crackling, and smoky, but they light easily and so make good kindling. The remainder are the hardwoods.

Most hardwoods burn fairly well, even elm and elder when really dry, but allowing for some exceptions due to situation and soil, the woods to leave alone when there are others to choose from are the eight shown here. Identify them by their leaves, and learn to know them by their bark. Ash is best of all.

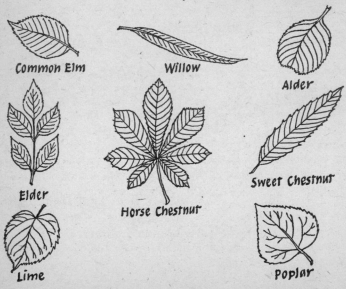

Common Elm

Willow

Alder

Elder

Horse Chestnut

Sweet Chestnut

Lime

Poplar

Why Wood Burns

A fireman puts a fire out by collapsing what he calls 'the fire triangle'. The three sides of the triangle represent air, heat, and burnable material. If any one of these is removed, the triangle collapses and the fire goes out.

The camper who wants to start a fire and keep it going, must build the triangle and keep all three sides strong enough to support it – an ample supply of oxygen (in the air), enough carbon (in the wood) and a sufficient temperature to keep the oxygen and carbon reacting and continuing to produce fire and flame.

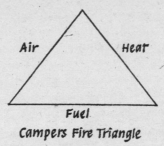

Campers Fire Triangle

Firelighting

Let us start by assuming that you have got permission to light a fire and to take dead wood, and that the choice is a hunter's fire. The plan of action is – select the site (preferably a bare patch to avoid cutting turf); find two logs (about 5 inches in diameter and poor burning wood, if possible), and fetch at least enough wood for the cooking job on hand (and the washing up); lay the fire and, when the cooking can start, light it.

The site should be fairly sheltered in case of high wind, and not where flying sparks could cause a fire, or where tree roots or peat could start an underground fire. A bare patch of ground is best for the hunter's fire, if it is intended to serve for any length of time, because the logs can be adjusted to suit any settled change of wind direction.

If the site is on grass, cut out a section of turf about 2 feet across and slightly longer than the logs, and at least 4 inches thick. If you have to use a knife instead of a spade or entrenching tool, and cannot cut and roll up the turf in one piece, cut it into foot-square sections. Place it grass upwards in a safe, shady place, for later replacement, and water well daily. Line the fire place with wood or stones to protect the grassy edges from damage.

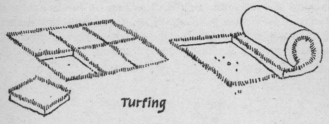

Turfing

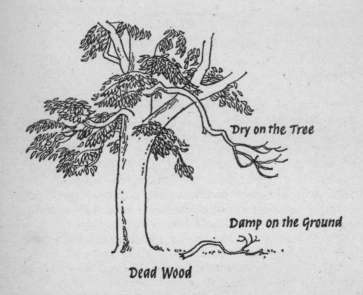

Dry on the Tree

Damp on the Ground

Dead Wood

Dry wood can nearly always be found on a tree, but rarely under it. Wood on the ground is almost always too damp to burn. Dead twigs and branches (look for withered leaves) can be broken or knocked off easily. This harmless operation can be mistaken for vandalism, so do get permission first. Wood supplies for weekend or longer camps should be cut to usable sizes and tidily stacked off the ground.

In laying a fire, the kindling (birch bark strips, pine, elder, or other twigs, no thicker than matchsticks) is all-important. It should be bunched loosely together, and sufficient to burn long enough to get the thicker sticks above it going well, and in turn the still thicker ones. Don't crowd the air out, and give the flames something to burn.

Laying a Fire

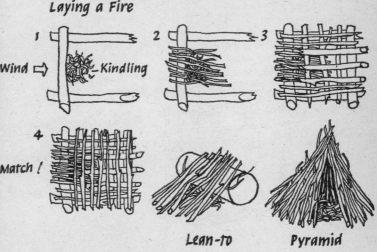

Light the fire on the windward side so that the first flames blow into the kindling. Strike the match close to the kindling, and let it burn half-way down before applying it.

Lighting an open-ground fire in a high wind, sit with your back to the wind and the fire between your legs.

A plate comes in useful for fanning the fire. Some campers use a metal-ended length of tubing to blow their fire up.

Pressure Stoves

There are three types of pressure stoves in general use today –
paraffin, petrol, and gas. All can be bought in models suitable
for hiking and lightweight camping, at between £5 and £9.

Paraffin: This is the type known to most as the 'primus', and
has many years of faithful service behind it. It is heavier than
the other two, and requires a separate fuel for priming, but it
is very efficient, the cheapest to run, and paraffin (kerosene)
is widely obtainable.

Petrol: Cleaner; quicker; needs no priming fuel, and some
models require no pumping. Petrol is dearer than paraffin and
riskier in camp.

Gas: Lightest in weight; clean; gives instant, finely regulated
heat; maintenance almost nil; but less power output than the

Parts of a Paraffin Pressure Stove

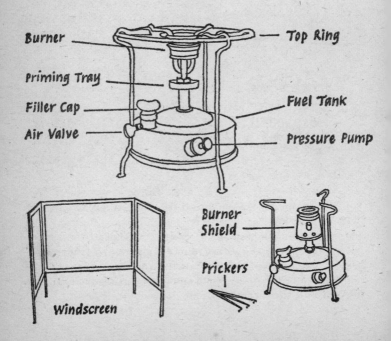

Burner — Top Ring

Priming Tray

Filler Cap — Fuel Tank

Air Valve — Pressure Pump

Burner Shield

Prickers

Windscreen

other two, and dearer to run.

How a paraffin pressure stove works: Liquid paraffin when heated vaporizes into a gas which, when ignited, gives off intense heat. A paraffin stove in action has the liquid at the bottom (in the tank) and the gas at the top (at the burner). In between, heated tubes are changing the liquid to gas. Pumped pressure keeps the paraffin flowing upwards through the heated tubes, and a tiny jet directs the ignited gas to the burner head. The heating tubes are kept hot by the flame.

To start a cold stove, the tubes must first be heated. That is why a priming (starting) fluid is necessary. It is lit in the circular tray under the burner tubes and there heats them up.

Here is the lighting drill, assuming that the stove is in order, the tank is three-quarters full, the jet is newly pricked clean, and the valve is open: put priming fuel in the tray and light it (always methylated, and preferably in solid form. A saucepan placed on the stove will help the heating of the burner tubes); when the fuel is almost burned out, close the valve, hold the stove steady, and give one or two short strokes of the pump. If a faint blue flame appears in the burner, all is well, so far. Give a full stroke or two and wait half a minute or so. If the blue flame increases, pump vigorously.

Should all not be well and the priming flame goes out, put a light to the burner. It will ignite if the priming fluid was sufficient. If not, refill tray and start again.

If, owing to pumping too much too soon, unvaporized paraffin produces an alarming yellow, sooty flame, open the valve at once and the flame will subside.

The valve is your 'on' and 'off' switch, as well as the flame regulator. Always leave it open when not in use.

The standard burner can be replaced by an extra-pressure 'roarer' burner for outdoor use, or by an adjustable, self-pricking burner.

Use nothing but paraffin to fuel a paraffin stove – never petrol. Store fuel airtight in a safe cool place away from food. Avoid using a pressure stove in a tent. A tent in flames may keep you warm for the moment, but it won't keep the rain out afterwards.

COOKING AND CATERING

COOKING food that makes enjoyable eating, and knowing what quantities to buy, comes with experience.

The camper new to cooking on a small stove or an open fire would do well to start with hardly any cooking at all. Be content at first with the achievement of lighting a fire (or stove) and keeping it going long enough to brew yourself a mug of drinkable tea or coffee to go with your sandwiches and fruit; and before turning in, making a cup of cocoa or heating a packet of soup; and next morning boiling an egg (and not forgetting the egg-cup and spoon) to follow the cereal and milk. Let the rest of the menu be as easy. Next time you will have enough confidence to be a little more ambitious.

. . . to be a little more ambitious

Always make the best use of your fire. Keep it as small as you need it – it saves wood. Don't waste heat. It can be heating washing-up water or keeping food or plates warm during a meal or before it is ready, either on the fire itself or on the tops of billies.

Be sure you don't run out of fuel before the cooking is finished. Cooking takes longer in camp than at home because heat in the open is not easily concentrated.

Get the right wood for the job, if you can. For boiling you want quick burning woods that give plenty of flame. For grilling, roasting, and stewing you need the slow-burning hardwoods. These also give you the hot glowing embers needed for frying, or ember or foil cooking.

Before you start a cooking job think out the right order of doing things. Note the cooking times given with recipes. For instance, if the sweet is going to take longer than the main course, it must be started before it. And time should be allowed for with the ingredients of a particular dish. For instance, carrots take longer to cook than potatoes, but the smaller either are cut the quicker they will cook, so you would cut the carrots smaller.

Remember also that appetites are bigger in camp than at home.

Food and Cooking

Wild animals eat all their food raw. We humans would be doing likewise had we not discovered that when raw food is heated beyond a certain temperature (about 65° C) it ceases to be the same thing merely warmed up. Instead, changes begin to take place which (generally) make it tastier and more enjoyable to eat and not just something to chew and swallow to satisfy hunger.

That discovery was the beginning of cooking. The different basic methods of cooking are simply the different ways of transferring heat of the right temperature, amount, and duration to produce the desired effect. For example, stewing is cooking in water just below boiling point (about 90°); steaming is cooking in steam over water at boiling point (100°); frying is cooking in contact with a hot surface (frying pan) or in oil or fat (about 175°); toasting, grilling, spit-roasting, are cooking close to fierce heat such as a fire (150°–205°); baking, oven-roasting, are cooking in hot air (230°–260°).

Why cook in different ways? – first, because some ways are more convenient than others, particularly in camp; and second (really more important than the first), different cooking methods produce different flavours and add variety to our eating. Almost the only reason for cooking food is to give it flavour that makes the eating a pleasure. There are hundreds of cookery books and thousands of recipes, each one somebody's way of imparting to food a particular flavour or combination of flavours.

Menus

More important than a food's flavour is its nutritional value. The feeling of hunger is your body's way of reminding you that it needs more food and it is time you stoked up. It doesn't tell you, at the time, what kinds it needs, but if it continually gets the wrong kinds, or the wrong quantities of the right kinds, you will find out eventually.

To be fit and well in camp or on the road, you should so plan your menus that they give you a balanced diet of the foods from the three groups the body needs. These are:

(a) the body building foods (proteins and mineral matter), which keep you growing and in good repair – meat, poultry, fish, eggs, cheese, milk, bread, cereals, peas, beans, nuts, etc.;

(b) energy foods (fats and carbohydrates), which provide body heat and the working energy needed for breathing, heartbeat and blood circulation, and all movement – butter, cheese, eggs, milk, sardines, bacon, ham, kippers, herrings, potatoes, most other vegetables, fruit, sugar, etc.;

(c) protective foods (vitamins), which keep you toned up and help you resist disease – you will have all you need if you include in your diet – milk, eggs, green vegetables, and fresh fruit.

Here are some suggestions to help you plan your menus. They are all simple dishes and within the scope of the beginner cook. Keep your menu within the limitations of your cooking gear. A breakfast of coffee, porridge, haddock, and stewed prunes, is a quick and easy cooking job until you try it with one billy and a lid.

Breakfast

Tea or coffee

and

porridge or cereal

and

eggs – boiled, poached, scrambled, or fried with bacon or tomatoes (or both) on fried bread (or not). Fried bacon and tomatoes with or without baked beans. Poached smoked haddock; fried herrings; kippers, boiled, fried, or planked. Fried sausage and tomatoes with or without baked beans. Cold boiled bacon or ham,

and

bread and butter with jam, marmalade, or honey. Fresh fruit or stewed apples, apricots, prunes, or other fruit. Dates, raisins, or nuts.

Dinner – midday or evening

Hotpot, liver and bacon, corned beef hash, Irish stew, sausage and mash. The following with potatoes and vegetables, or (with the fried meats) fried onions or tomatoes, or both – stewed or fried steak; beef or mutton, boiled, or pot-roasted with root vegetables; lamb cutlets; fried pork chops; white fish (cod, haddock, plaice, etc.)

followed by

pancakes, milk pudding, bread and butter pudding, plum duff, stewed fruit – apples, apricots, gooseberries, pears, plums, prunes, rhubarb – and custard; fresh fruit.

Lunch or Tea

Pressed beef, ham, tongue, corned beef, or spam – with potatoes (boiled or fried) or tomatoes (raw or fried) or both, – or with mixed or green salad. Mixed or green salad with sardines, or sliced hard-boiled eggs and grated cheese. Welsh rarebit, toasted cheese and tomatoes or bacon, or both. Sandwiches (sliced loaf easiest) – boiled beef, ham, tongue, sausage, sardines, chopped hard-boiled egg with chutney or mayonnaise, grated or cream cheese with chopped dates, celery, cucumber, and onion, or sliced tomato; potted meat, paste – shrimp, fish, meats, etc. Most sandwiches are improved by adding salad fillings such as lettuce, watercress, mustard and cress, and sliced cucumber.

(Some of the dishes suggested for breakfasts are suitable for lunch or tea, with tea or coffee, and, if required, followed by fresh or stewed fruit, or bread, butter and jam, marmalade or honey.)

Supper

Cocoa and biscuits, or soup (packet or tin) and biscuits or bread.

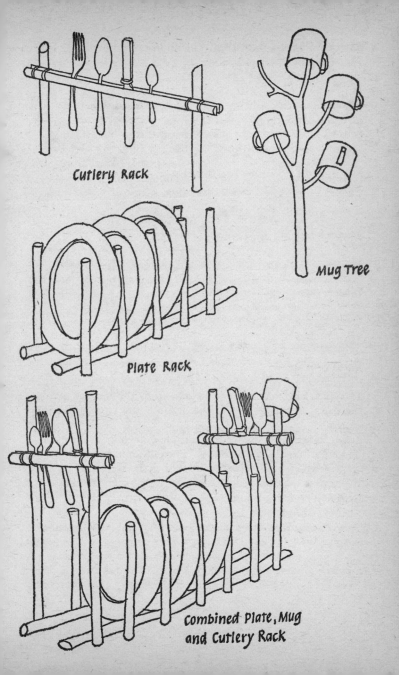

Cutlery Rack

Mug Tree

Plate Rack

Combined Plate, Mug
and Cutlery Rack

Average Food Quantities

for two campers for one day

Bacon, ham, etc., 4 oz
Biscuits, plain, 6 oz
Bread, 2 lb
Butter or margarine, 4 oz
Cake, slab, 4 oz
Cheese, 4 oz
Cocoa, ½ oz
Coffee – ground (two ½-pints), 2 oz
Coffee – instant (two ½-pints), ¼ oz
Fat, cooking, 1 oz
Fish, ¾ lb
Fruit – fresh, ¾ lb

Jam or marmalade, 4 oz
Meat – frying, roasting, ¾ lb
Meat – stewing, ½ lb
Milk, 1 pint
Oatmeal or cereal, 4 oz
Potatoes, 1 lb
Rice, 3 oz
Salt, ½ oz
Sausage, ¾ lb
Sugar, 6 oz
Tea (for six ½ pints), ½ oz
Tomatoes, ¾ lb
Vegetables, green or root, 1 lb

Food Storage

In camp, food has to be protected from the heat of the day, the damp in the air and in the ground, and from insects and animals.

Heat: The coolest places are – the shade, a hole in the ground, and cold water. The store tent (if any) should be in the shade, with its walls brailed (rolled up and tied). If it is a ridge tent that opens at both ends and has a fly-sheet, so much the better. The tent should, if possible, be sited where it will be in the shade all day.

A hole in the ground makes a good larder. In hot weather it is cooler in the ground than on it. Like the store tent, it should be in continual shade. Its size will be according to the needs, but it should be deep enough for its contents (which might well be eggs, milk, butter, or other fats) to be completely below ground level. Give any insect- or animal-protection necessary, such as a large polythene bag or small ones, and with a few interlaced sticks and grass or bracken make a cover for it. Greenstuff keeps the heat out. Mark the spot to avoid broken legs or broken eggs.

Cold water and muslin provide an effective cooling method. For example, milk in a bottle or other container is stood in about an inch of water, then the muslin is wetted through and draped over the container, clinging to it with its ends lying in the water. As the moisture in the muslin evaporates and cools the container, water creeps up the muslin keeping it moist.

Other foodstuffs can lie under moist muslin above water level on a stone or brick, or in a dish. A running stream is a good cooler.

Damp: Dampness in the air will get wherever air can get, so anything that would be the worse for it, such as biscuits, sugar, and particularly salt (very hygroscopic), should be kept airtight in rigid containers or polythene bags. Label where necessary. Keep things off the ground, and guard against tent leaks.

Insects and animals: Muslin will keep insects off foods which need air, such as meat, sausage, bacon, and fish, but it must not be touching the food at any point, otherwise it can still be contaminated through the muslin. Such foods are better in an improvised meat-safe hanging at a safe height in a tree, rather than at ground level inviting foxes, cats, dogs, and farm animals.

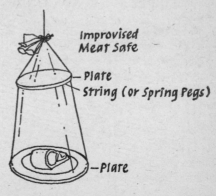

Improvised
Meat Safe

— Plate
String (or Spring Pegs)

— Plate

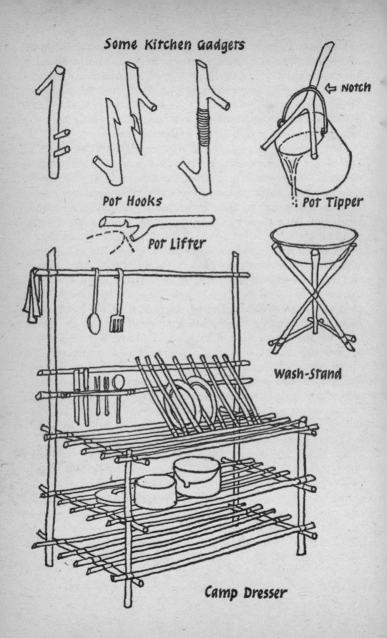

Some Kitchen Gadgets

← Notch

Pot Hooks

Pot Tipper

Pot Lifter

Wash-Stand

Camp Dresser

Store tent: Keep only food in the store tent – certainly not the smelly first-aid box. Foodstuffs which pick up other flavours, such as eggs, should be kept away from cheese, onions, kippers, and the like. Leave no uneaten food about, and wipe jam and butter pots clean. Do nothing to encourage insects or animals.

When there is no store tent, food should be kept in a suitable and safe place outside, not in a sleeping tent.

In hot weather, meat and similar perishables should be cooked as soon as possible, either for eating immediately, or later in cold meals. Part-cooking meat to prevent it 'going off' can actually hasten it (especially pork) and cause food poisoning. When possible, buy perishable foodstuffs in minimum quantities, and as near to time of use as you can. Meat in foods such as sausage rolls will go bad if stored in airtight containers.

Milk goes sour quickly in containers with even the slightest trace of previous contents, so thoroughly clean and scald out before each new supply. New milk mixed with old goes sour quickly.

Bacon, cheese, butter, and other fats are best left in their wrappers. They may be further wrapped in foil, or put in polythene bags, closed but not airtight. Bread will keep well in a polythene bag so long as air can get in – and insects cannot. Biscuits should be stored airtight and alone. Stored with bread or cake they take their moisture and go soft. A lump or two of sugar in a biscuit container keeps the biscuits dry by absorbing any moisture present. It is not unsafe to leave food in an opened can.

Keep drinking-water covered and in the shade.

Tube foods: The range of foods which can be bought in tubes now includes condensed milk, jam, marmalade, cheese, fruit purées, jellies, tomato purée, meat and fish pastes, and mustard, and are worth keeping in mind. They can be a useful standby in case of need; they ease the catering and storage problem for the lightweight camper, particularly on sites miles from shop or farm; and they are economical and keep fresh to the last squeeze.

The Cooking Place

If the cooking is to be done on a stove, almost any place will do, so long as the stove is sheltered, stands firm and solid, and is not inside or too near a tent or anything else that could catch fire. With an open fire, wind direction decides its position. In a hike-camp or weekend camp, the fire would not be sited where the smoke was a nuisance, or flying sparks dangerous. In a standing-camp, wind direction not only decides the position of the kitchen within the camp but also the fire within the kitchen and the rest of the kitchen layout.

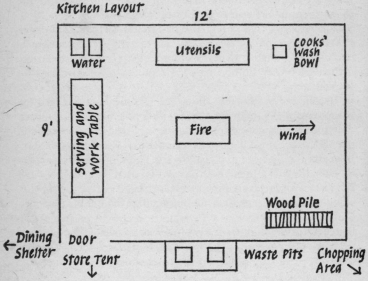

Kitchen Layout

The size of a kitchen, its various parts and equipment will depend on the size of the camp, but in addition to the fireplace it will at least have a wet pit with a grease cover for straining liquids through, and a dry pit for unburnable rubbish. It might also have a table for preparing and serving food, a cook's wash bowl, a washing-up bench, and a wood stack. Whatever its size, it should always be roped off and made taboo to all but cooks and helpers, to lessen the risk of accidents, particularly scaldings.

Wet and dry pits: Where there is cooking there are waste solids and waste water to be disposed of – and there are flies looking for smelly places to breed in. So, burn everything burnable, unless the farmer wants your peelings and scraps for his pigs. Ask him about rubbish disposal before digging his ground up. He may prefer to lend you a sack and use his own rubbish dump for unburnable rubbish. Keep such a sack closed and off the ground.

Wet pit: This must be completely efficient to be of any use at all, and that simply means that nothing goes into the pit but strained liquid. If solids can get in, so can flies.

The pit should be about a foot deep and a foot square, and covered with a firm lacework of sticks about 2 inches apart. This is then given a good filter cover of long grass, bracken, or the like. Waste liquids are poured on to it, grease and solids stay on the top and the clear liquid filters through into the pit and soaks away into the ground. The filter-cover should be renewed and the soiled one burned at least twice a day. Other means of supporting the filter-cover can be used, such as wire netting on a frame, or an old sieve or riddle, or a perforated biscuit tin standing in a pit its own size and filled with grass or other natural filter material, which is regularly burned.

Dry pit: This is the same size as the wet pit, unless the farmer wants it deeper. It is for unburnable rubbish such as tin cans. Cans are first burned out to remove all traces of food, and flattened to save space in the pit. Aerosol and similar containers will explode if thrown on to the fire, so flatten and cover with soil in the pit. Dry pits need not be covered.

Wet Pit with Grease Trap

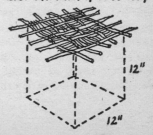

12"

12"

Location: Wet and dry pits are best located just outside the kitchen but reachable from inside, and roped off unless they happen to be between the kitchen and a hedge. Efficient pits, like efficient latrines, do not need disinfectant.

Some Camp Cookery

TEA

To make tea the water must be boiling. It will taste better if the water is allowed to boil for only the few seconds it takes to put the tea in, and if it is drunk soon after it has brewed.

1 Measure required amount of water into billy – say, a $\frac{1}{2}$-pint mugful per person.
2 Put water on to boil.
3 Measure tea into dry mug – a heaped teaspoon per two mugs.
4 Watch water. At point of boiling (when bubbling) tip tea in and at once remove billy from fire.
5 Cover billy and let stand for 5 minutes. Then milk and sweeten tea in billy or in mugs, and pour.

COFFEE

Ways of making coffee and the quantity to use vary with different brands and types, and with the people who drink it. Instant coffee is made in the same way as tea, and can be made in individual mugs. Making ground coffee is normally a less straightforward business, but there are ways of making it in a billy and cutting out the coffee pot or jug normally required.

Perhaps the best way, because only one billy is needed, is to make it in exactly the same way as already described for making tea, keeping in mind the essentials – coffee tipped in as soon as the water is at the boil; billy at once withdrawn from fire or stove, and allowed to stand covered for 5 minutes. To sink any floating grounds stir for a moment or sprinkle a few drops of cold water in. Milk and sweeten in billy or mugs. Pour carefully and the grounds will stay at the bottom. A pinch of salt added to the dry coffee improves the flavour. Two heaped dessertspoonsful of ground coffee per $\frac{1}{2}$ pint of water, or a heaped teaspoonful of instant coffee, is the normal amount.

COCOA

Follow the instructions on the label, but always use milk when you can. It makes a much more satisfying and nourishing drink than when made with water.

PORRIDGE

Patent brands: follow instructions on packet.

Coarse oatmeal: soak overnight in cold water, two handfuls to a pint of water (for two single helpings). Next morning add a teaspoonful of salt. Put over heat, bring to the boil, then allow to simmer for about 20 minutes, frequently stirring.

Rolled oats: Bring water to the boil, sprinkle oats in, keep boiling for 5 minutes, stirring constantly. Quantities (including salt) as for coarse meal, or varied as required.

Serve hot, with hot or cold milk, sugar or syrup, or salt only.

EGGS

Boiled: Lower carefully into boiling water sufficient to cover. Keep gently boiling (rapid boiling cracks) for 4 to 5 minutes for moderately soft; about 3 to $3\frac{1}{2}$ minutes for soft boiled; and 8 to 10 minutes for hard. Have your bread already cut and buttered.

Poached: Bring water to the boil in a half-filled pan, deep or shallow so long as it has a lid. Break each egg into the boiling water, then put lid on and remove pan from heat. The eggs will go on cooking and will be ready in about 3 minutes. Remove and serve on buttered toast already waiting.

Scrambled: Allow two or more eggs per person. Break them into a mug or bowl, preferably each into something separate first to prevent a possible bad one spoiling the others. Add a little salt and pepper and beat the eggs with a fork until thoroughly mixed. Put butter (a teaspoonful per two eggs) into a small pan (ideal if the mixture half fills it) and place over a low heat. When the butter begins to froth, pour the eggs in and stir continuously, keeping the whole mixture on the move. It is cooked when it is no longer liquid and not yet dry. Goes well with buttered toast.

BACON AND EGGS

As it matters little whether the bacon is put in a cold or heated frying pan, put it in cold because it is easier to arrange.

1 Lightly grease frying pan. (No grease necessary when frying bacon only.)
2 Cut rind off rashers and lay in pan. If rashers have to overlap let fat part be touching pan, because it takes longer to cook than lean.
3 Put pan on fire (not too hot a flame) and let the bacon sizzle for a minute or two. When it changes colour turn over and cook other side.
4 When it is cooked, remove the rashers (allowing each to drip its fat back into the pan) and place where they will keep hot – on a covered plate over a steaming billy, for example, otherwise leave piled at one side of frying pan (if room) and kept off direct heat of fire.
5 Add fat to pan, if required. There should be enough for basting (spooning fat over) the eggs.
6 Break each egg into a mug and pour gently into pan. If no mug handy, break directly into pan.
7 Baste eggs until yolks film over white and set. Serve with bacon.

SAUSAGES – FRIED

Sausages should be cooked slowly (about 10 minutes) over low heat. It prevents bursting and burning. Pricking is not necessary. They burst only when heated too quickly.

1 Separate the sausages, if linked, and put in a cold frying pan, lightly greased.
2 Place pan on fire. Keep sausages just sizzling, and turn as each side browns.

TOMATOES

Fried tomatoes go well with sausages and take about as long to cook. They also make a tasty addition to fried bacon or egg, or both, or alone on fried bread or toast, seasoned with salt and pepper.

1   Cut tomatoes in half, crossways. Place face down in greased
    frying pan.
2   After a minute or two, turn tomatoes face uppermost.
3   Salt lightly, and cook until skins soften and wrinkle.

KIPPERS

Kippers require little cooking because the process of kippering
makes them eatable even if uncooked.
Boiled: Bring water to the boil in a frying pan or billy, enough
to cover the kippers. Put kippers in and immediately remove
pan from fire. Let stand in the off-the-boil water for 3 or 4
minutes and they are ready for eating.
Planked: This is a form of roasting. The kipper is opened out
flat and fixed to a piece of wood (plank) or something similar
in shape, and propped up close to the fire. It is done when the
skin begins to shrivel. Cook only on the one side, preferably the
inside. A hot fire with little flame and smoke is required.
Fried: Fry in a little fat, one side only, for about 5 minutes
over a moderate fire.

SMOKED HADDOCK – POACHED

Remove tail, and corners at head. Cut into portions if too large
to lie flat in pan. Place in pan, cover with water, put lid on.
Bring to boil. At boiling point remove from heat, and leave to
cool slowly for 10 minutes with lid on.

POTATOES – BOILED

Peel or scrape. Cut large ones in half or smaller. Potatoes or
pieces of the same size take the same time to cook and so are
ready together. Put them in the smallest pan that will hold
them, and cover with water. (The less water the less flavour
loss). Remove the potatoes. Add salt – a heaped teaspoonful
to 2 lb of potatoes. Bring water to the boil, add the potatoes,
put lid on, and keep water boiling fast until done – about 20
minutes.

For mashed potatoes, cut to Oxo-cube size. Time – about
10 minutes; fried: boil until nearly done. Remove and slice.
Fry in a little butter.

VEGETABLES

In general, vegetables should be cooked as fast as possible, and in as little water as possible. Prolonged heat destroys the vitamins, so the less time the cooking takes the better. Water robs the vegetable of flavour and goodness, so the less water the better.

For example, to cook a cabbage, cut it down the centre into four and remove the hard centre parts. Cut the leaves into shreds. (They cook faster being in smaller pieces.) Wash the shredded leaves. Put about an inch of water into a billy and add a little salt. Bring to the boil, add the cabbage, put lid on, and boil really fast. Keep boiling and stir occasionally. Cooking time: about 10 minutes.

STEW

Stews are very nourishing because none of the goodness in the ingredients is lost, and none of it is destroyed by boiling. A stew should never be allowed to boil. Boiling toughens meat, but slow moist heat (simmering) tenderizes it.

IRISH STEW

For two portions you need 1 lb scrag end of mutton or 4 mutton chops, 1 lb potatoes, 1 large onion.

Cut the meat into small pieces (if chops, leave whole), peel potatoes and onions and cut into slices.

Tip ingredients into a billy with just enough water to cover, and add a heaped teaspoonful of salt. Cover billy.

Put on a slow fire or stove, bring almost to the boil and allow to simmer a little below boiling point for 2 hours from time of reaching full heat.

Almost any vegetables can go into a stew – carrots, turnips, leeks, tomatoes, celery, herbs, spices, canned peas, canned baked beans.

INSTANT STEW

Canned meat, canned vegetables, and canned soup, tipped into a billy and heated up.

FRIED STEAK

1 lb for two portions – fillet, sirloin, or rump. Not stewing steak.

Grease frying pan, and get it very hot. Put the steak in and keep the pan hot. Cook each side 3 to 5 minutes, according to thickness. If cooking with onions, chop them up and put them in the pan first. When they begin to brown, put the steak in. Tomatoes can be added if desired.

CHOPS

These can be cooked in a frying pan in the same way as fried steak and with the same additions. Turn them over occasionally while frying. They take about the same time.

PANCAKES

For two portions: 1 egg, 3 oz flour (4 heaped dessertspoonsful, or a ½-pint mug half filled), ¼ pint milk. Put flour into mug or bowl. Make hollow in middle of flour and break egg into it. Pour in a little milk and begin beating with a fork. Go on adding milk gradually as you beat and continue until the whole is thoroughly mixed and without lumps.

Put pan over a good heat, with just enough fat in to coat the bottom. Pour in enough mixture (batter) to cover the pan bottom thinly. Shake or tilt pan to spread it.

The underside of the batter is done as soon as a sharp shake of the pan dislodges it in one piece. Turn the pancake over and cook other side for same length of time.

Serve with jam, or sprinkling of sugar and lemon juice, and rolled.

MILK PUDDING

For two portions: Rice – 3 oz (4 rounded dessertspoonsful), sugar – 2 dessertspoonsful, milk – 1 pint.

Put milk into billy. Bring to boil with lid on. Put rice and sugar into boiling milk, and at once stir for a moment to prevent rice sticking. Replace lid and keep just boiling for about 20 minutes or until tender. Serve plain or with stewed fruit or jam.

STEWED FRESH FRUIT

Apples or pears should be peeled and cut up into small pieces, and rhubarb (cut ends off, but do not skin if young) is cut into 1- to 2-inch pieces. Small fruit, such as damsons, cherries, gooseberries are cooked whole. Plums and apricots can be halved. Do not stone any fruit.

Put an inch of water in billy and add 4 dessertspoonsful of sugar for each pound of fruit. Bring to the boil. Add fruit and simmer slowly for about 20 minutes. Fruit acidity varies, so if more sugar is required, add after cooking.

STEWED DRIED FRUIT

Soak overnight in water just covering, with lid on. Cook, in the same water, at just below boiling point for about 20 minutes.

Backwoods Cookery

This is cookery without utensils. Useful in an emergency or for managing with less cooking gear on a hike.

GREENSTICK COOKING

The food is cooked on a stick held or propped near the fire. The stick should be peeled clean and baked dry, and just before use should be made hot to help cook the centre of anything wrapped round it or impaled on it. One end can be pointed if foods have to be pierced. Finger thickness is a good size. Choose ash, beech, oak, or other wood that is not sweet or bitter smelling.

Twists: A form of camp bread. Required, for four twists – a ½-pint mug half full of self-raising flour, a pinch of salt, and water – and a red-ember fire.

Make a hollow in the mug of flour, add the salt and gradually add water, stirring with a thin stick or spoon handle until you have a firm paste. Take out a lump of the dough, roll it into a narrow strip and wrap it round the heated stick, each turn slightly overlapping so that when it is done it can be slit open like a roll and have a filling of butter, jam, fried bacon, or anything you like.

Place near fire, and occasionally turn to bake all sides. It is done when it sounds hollow, and no longer clings to the stick.

Kabobs: This is a mixed grill. Assemble on the stick small (about 1 inch square) pieces of any meat or vegetables at hand – mutton, onion, bacon, mushroom, kidney, tomato, sausage, potato – and cook over hot fire, turning as it cooks.

BROILER COOKING

The broiler is a forked stick with other sticks interwoven, or any similar gadget that can be used as a portable grill.

Cheese Dreams: This is really a grilled cheese sandwich which becomes a backwoodsman's Welsh rarebit. The sandwich can be made from two separate slices in the usual way, but it is better if one piece is cut twice as thick, sliced open along one side, and the cheese slices or pieces inserted. It is then toasted both sides over a hot fire, secured in the broiler.

Almost anything else grillable can be cooked in the same way – steak, chops, sausage (best spiked), fish.

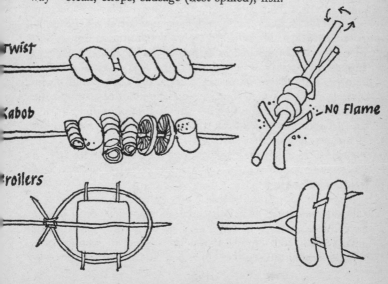

Twist

Kabob

Broilers

No Flame

EMBER COOKING

A fire deep in embers is needed so that they can be built around or over the foodstuff.

Baked potatoes: Cover the unpeeled potato with embers and leave for about 45 minutes. When done (test with knife or fork whether soft) scrape away blackened part. Cut in half and mix some butter in. Add grated cheese, if desired.

Alternatively, first wrap potato tightly in wet paper, or coat with clay or wet earth. Other root vegetables – carrots, onions, turnips – can be baked in the same way, apples too.

Ember bread: Make dough as for twist, take a lump and make an inch-thick, round shape of it. Clear a bare space in the embers, place the dough on it and cover with hot embers. Baking time about 15 minutes. Scrape clean and eat buttered while warm.

HOT STONE COOKING

A flat stone is heated in a very hot fire, and the stone is used for frying on. Flint should not be used – it explodes.

Fried egg and bacon: Wipe stone clean. Make a square or triangle of fairly thick slices of bacon, leaving sufficient space for an egg to be broken into it. When cooked, eat it off the stone. Alternatively, a slice of bread with a hole in the middle can be placed over the bacon (or without the bacon) and the egg broken into that.

Damper: Another form of camp bread. Mix the dough as for a twist, make a 1-inch thick, round shape out of a lump of it. Place it on the hot stone. Give it about 5 minutes on each side. If a second stone is kept hot, the damper can be transferred to it for baking the other side.

Haybox Cooking

The haybox is an insulated container. It works on a similar principle to a thermos flask. In fact, a thermos flask can do many of the cooking jobs that a haybox can do, though on a smaller scale.

A haybox does not actually cook anything, but it retains heat so long that the effect on what is put into it is the same as leaving it on a fire that is very slowly burning out. That is why, for instance, a stew (which is cooked by simmering) when put into a haybox at boiling point will go on simmering long enough to be cooked through. Porridge that has been put in at boiling point the night before is ready for eating at breakfast time.

Hay (and some modern substitutes), having insulating properties which prevent the normal transfer of heat, forms the lining of the box and so keeps the heat in.

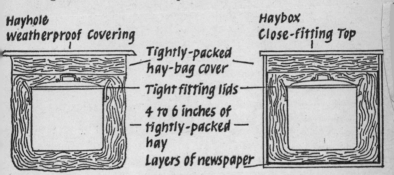

Hayhole
Weatherproof Covering

Tightly-packed
hay-bag cover

Tight fitting lids

4 to 6 inches of
tightly-packed
hay

Layers of newspaper

Haybox
Close-fitting Top

A hayhole, on the same principle, can be made in the ground.
Foil: Aluminium foil is very useful in camp – food storage, cooking, improvising utensils, keeping sandwiches fresh on hikes, and many other uses. It is ideal for cooking in hot embers and can withstand any amount of cooking heat. It needs to be protected only from flames, which have a melting effect on it.

Foil takes up little space, weighs hardly anything and with care can be used again and again.

KNIVES, AXES, AND SAWS

THE experienced camper, like the skilled craftsman, knows that to get good and long service out of his tools he must properly use, maintain, and care for them.

Knives

Clasp knife or sheath knife? The merits of both are still argued about.

The clasp knife with attachments, such as tin- and bottle-opener, is a compact multi-purpose tool that can be easily stowed away in rucksack or pocket, or kept on belt swivel. To be useful to camper or hiker, it should have a 5-inch blade (a good size for cutting bread) and at least a tin-opener and marline spike. Other attachments, and a second blade (kept for special jobs), add little to its bulk and weight. A good-quality knife of this kind costs between £1 and £3.50.

A sheath knife is a knife and nothing more, but it is handier than a clasp knife. It does not need both hands to bring it into use, and it can be applied at any angle without fear of the blade doubling back on to your fingers. The Bushman's Friend type of knife, with its 5-inch, flat, broadish blade, is a useful camp knife and costs about £1.20. A knife with a hilt prevents the hand slipping on to the blade. The sheath should have a secure means of preventing the knife dropping out, and

Clasp Knife

Sheath Knife (Bushman's Friend)

is best worn towards the back, clear of the swing of the arm.

Oil your knife occasionally, and keep it sharp. There are several ways of sharpening a knife. Here is one effective method, using a round carborundum stone. Hold the stone with its rough side up. Now, with the blade almost flat, push the edge along the stone, from point to base, in a circular movement away from you. After several strokes, in the outward direction only, turn the blade over and reverse the movement (base to point) for the same number of strokes. Then do the same lightly on the finer side of the stone, to remove the burr.

Perhaps the answer to the clasp-knife versus sheath-knife question is to have a clasp knife for its attachments and for rough work like turfing, and a sheath knife for other purposes.

Axes

The hand axe most popular with campers, and which has proved itself the most suitable for cutting small timber, is the type known to foresters as the hunter's hatchet. It is like a small-scale felling axe. The haft is about 12 to 16 inches long, and the head weighs 1 to 3 lb.

Two varieties of this pattern of axe are: a bonded (wedge-less) type; and an all-steel, one-piece type with handle grip of rubber, wood, or plastic. This steel model is, size for size, heavier than the wooden-hafted type (one 13½-inch model weighs

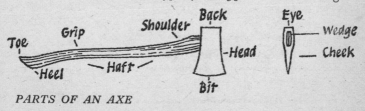

PARTS OF AN AXE

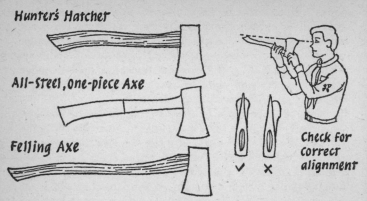

Hunter's Hatchet

All-Steel, One-piece Axe

Felling Axe

Check for correct alignment

29 oz, compared with 25 oz) but it is no more expensive and should give long service, free from trouble with wedges and loose heads.

The felling axe varies more in weight and length than in style. Lengths of hafts are from about 24 to 36 inches, and weight of heads from about $2\frac{1}{2}$ to 7 lb.

Buying an axe needs to be done with care, especially the wooden-hafted kind, because a haft of faulty fit or poor quality can cause a serious accident. The head should fit tight. The haft should be of hickory or ash. Hickory is tougher than ash, and is the most shock-resistant of all timbers. The grain must run straight down the length of the haft, or it will split in use. There should be no knots. Cheap hafts are usually painted to hide their faults. Check that the head is correctly aligned. Hold it, blade uppermost, and look along the cutting edge. It should be in line with the heel of the haft.

Look after your axe. Don't chop through wood into the

Honing   **Grinding**   **Keep Wet**

ground. Keep your axe clean and sharp. Make a habit of always hand-honing it after use, and there will seldom be any need to put it to a grindstone. Use a smooth hard whetstone, rubbing equally along the entire edge of the bevel, holding the head with the cutting edge uppermost and making the strokes away from you. Give both sides the same treatment, retaining the original convex shape of the blade.

Keep the head thinly greased (vaseline will do). Put a smear on the cutting edge itself – rust flecks dull a blade's keenness. Occasionally rub linseed oil thinly into the haft. Do not sharpen an axe with a file; it gives a rough edge.

If an axe head becomes loose in storage, as happens when too dry conditions reduce the natural moisture content of the haft, immerse the head and haft in a bucket of water for a few hours.

Treat your axe with respect. Never play the fool with it.

Saws

Saws in camp are gradually ousting the felling axe. Sawing is tidier, faster, and less wasteful of wood and energy.

The types most commonly seen in camp are: the folding saw, about 20 inches folded length, and packs safely in a rucksack; the bandsaw – a length of toothed steel wire with finger-rings at each end; and the bow (or bush) saw – a steel, bowed frame, and a narrow blade.

The folding saw (really a pruning saw) can do much of the work a hand axe does. The bandsaw does light work and usually requires an extra pair of hands. The bow saw can do all the

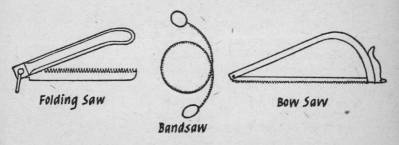

Folding Saw

Bandsaw

Bow Saw

light and medium work of the felling axe, and the heavier work of the hand axe.

Saws are not likely to oust the hand axe. All its work can normally be coped with single-handed and, unlike the saw, nothing is too small for it.

Bow saws are in sizes according to the length of the blade. The biggest for one-man use has a 36-inch blade. A 24-inch costs about £3.40, and a spare blade, 85p. There are saws with adjustable frames.

After use, a saw should have its teeth cleaned (an old toothbrush is appropriate) and given a smearing of oil (a soft brush makes this job easier). Masking can be done by wrapping a strip of suitable fabric spirally round the blade.

Modern blades, with specially hardened teeth, give such good service that it is cheaper to buy a new blade than to have a worn one doctored.

Safety with an Axe

An axe is a useful tool, but a dangerous one in inexperienced or careless hands. Be safety minded.

AXES IN GENERAL
Before using
    Check that the axe is sharp, and the head not loose
    Wear no loose clothing. Remove lanyards, etc.
    See clearly what you are doing, in good light and out of
        smoke
    Do not wear gloves if they are likely to become slippery
While using
    Grip the axe firmly and keep control throughout the stroke
    If the axe head becomes loose, stop at once
    If you tire, take a rest
    Keep your eye on what you are doing
    Do not become over-confident or careless
After using
    Do not leave an axe propped up anywhere, or lying on the
        ground
    Never throw an axe

Always mask when not in use, in its case, or in sacking, or with the bit completely buried in a log or stump

HAND AXES IN PARTICULAR

Keep onlookers at least 6 feet away

Chop sticks downwards, away from the body

Do not lean sticks against anything to chop them. Flying sticks are dangerous

FELLING AXES IN PARTICULAR

Keep onlookers at least two axe lengths (the reach of an axe held at arm's length) away

Clear the ground where working, and the area of the axe swing. Even a twig can dangerously deflect a swinging axe

Wear walking shoes for firmer stance and better foot protection, rather than canvas shoes

Do not use an axe in rain. A slippery grip is dangerous, and so is slippery bark and wood

Give warning of a falling tree

Never stand behind anybody who is using an axe

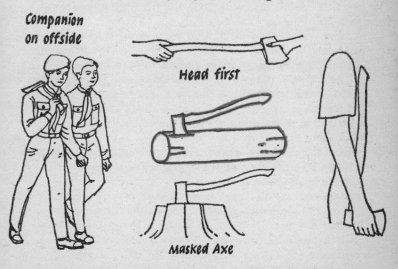

Companion on offside

Head first

Masked Axe

Using Felling Axe and Saw

To fell a tree with an axe the trunk is chopped about half-way through from one side, then half-way through from the other side, and the tree falls. Then, as it lies on the ground, the trunk is trimmed of its branches. Next, the trunk is cut up into logs. These are the three operations foresters call felling, trimming, and logging up.

When an axeman comes to fell a tree there are several things he considers before going into action.

Before felling he must decide which way the tree is to fall. His first choice would be the direction in which it would naturally tend to fall, so long as there were no obstructions and it did not fall across a ditch or stream, making trimming or logging up difficult. He would fell uphill rather than downhill because of the possible danger of rolling. In windy conditions he would not fell, especially a tree in full leaf.

Felling, he would start by chopping out a kerf on the side of the tree facing the intended direction of the fall, cutting just more than half-way through the tree with alternate sideways and downward diagonal strokes. Then he would start another kerf a little higher up on the opposite side of the tree, and when he had cut through to the first kerf the tree would fall, its direction being at right angles to the kerf-line.

The felling-axe stroke (which should be well practised first, perhaps with a specially adapted cast-out broom) is made by holding the grip of the haft firmly in the left hand, and with the right hand holding the haft loosely at its shoulder. With both feet comfortably apart and planted squarely, raise the head of the axe back over your right shoulder, and as you bring it down to strike let your right hand slide down the haft to meet your left hand at the end of the stroke. Stand loose and relaxed, and do not move your feet. Practise striking left-handed. It is sometimes needed. When the bit sticks, release it by a downward tap on the haft, or by an up-and-down movement – never sideways.

Let the axe do most of the work. Powerful strokes are not necessary with a sharp axe. Work Study has shown that a 3-lb

Felling

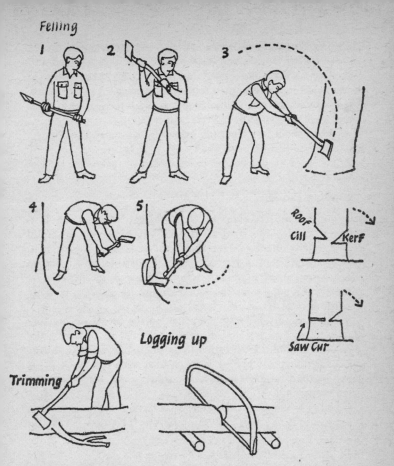

1
2
3
4
5

Roof
Cill Kerf

Saw Cut

Trimming

Logging up

axe is as efficient as a 7-lb axe, and requires less effort.

Felling by saw requires only a front kerf. This can be cut entirely by saw, or by axe after sawing the cill. Next saw from the other side through to the kerf. A wooden or metal wedge should be driven in behind the blade to prevent jambing and to help throw the tree over.

After felling, let the tree settle before starting work on it.

When trimming, work from butt to tip of tree, chopping at the undersides of the branches and working with the grain.

137

Keep the trunk between you and the side you are trimming.

Logging up with a saw is easier, quicker, tidier, and less wasteful of wood than with an axe. Logs should be supported underneath to prevent saw blade or axe biting into the ground. Logging with an axe, cut half-way through the log with wide-angle V-cuts, then turn the log over and repeat.

Timber should be stacked according to size and so that air can circulate through the stack.

Chopping Wood

Firewood should be chopped only where it is safe to chop it. (Remember the safety rules.) In standing-camps there should be a specially allocated area about 10 yards from the kitchen, to leeward. It should be roped off, if possible, and taboo to others when an axeman is in action. There should be a chopping block, or log, and the wood should be stacked, roughly according to size.

Chop sticks by holding them flat on the block and making the stroke away from you at about 45° (diagonally across the grain), or by holding the stick at an angle and striking downwards at the spot where it is in contact with the block. This latter method requires a more accurate stroke, but it is made at an easier angle.

Thicker wood is cut through by alternate diagonal strokes cutting into each other and chipping out the wood.

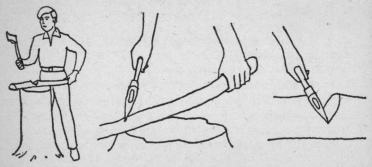

Chopping heavier wood on the ground, plant your feet firmly apart and chop with a steady rhythm.

A sharp axe, well directed, will do most of the work for you. Heavy blows are not necessary. Practise accurate chopping.

Whittling

To be able to make a tent peg in case of need, or a pot-hook or other gadgetry, can help with the smooth running of camp and add to its comfort.

All that is needed is a really sharp knife and a bit of practice. You might eventually rise to carving a totem pole.

Here are a few guiding pointers. The rest is up to you and your imagination, and practice.

A sharp knife is safer to use than a blunt one. Practise on soft woods – pines, firs, cedar. Willow is also good. Later, choose the wood suitable for the job. For example, a hard wood such as ash, oak, beech, sycamore, for a tent peg.

Hold the wood in your left hand (reverse if left-handed), just below where you intend to cut. As you apply the knife to the wood, keep your left thumb against your right thumb (which is on the back of the blade) so that they work together in controlling the blade as well as adding pressure to the cutting.

Hold wood and knife firmly and make all cuts away from the body, if possible. If you have to make cuts towards the body, hold the wood at chest level, and as you apply the knife, rest your right thumb on the wood as a steadying support and brake, and (if you want extra support) place your left thumb on your right.

The natural shape of the wood you select, and use of the axe, can give you a good start.

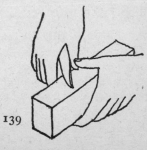

KNOTS AND LASHINGS

MOST of us tie knots almost every day of our lives. We tie our shoe laces and our ties without thinking about it. Scaffolders, packers, weavers, firemen, farmers, nurses, sailors, and others could not do their jobs without tying knots.

The camper with a few knots at his fingertips adds to his comfort and the smooth-running of camp. He might wish to keep his meat safe up in a tree (clove hitch); or to join a rope to another (sheet bend); or to improvise a broken or lost runner (guy-line hitch); or to finish off a bandage or sling (reef knot). If he knows a lashing or two, for binding things together, he can make better gadgets for his comfort, or have a go at building a bridge over a stream to short-cut the farm or village.

About Rope

Vegetable fibres are still the commonest materials for rope making, although synthetic fibres, such as nylon and terylene are being used more and more. Nylon makes the strongest of all ropes, but its elasticity, though just what the climber needs for withstanding sudden shock loading, is a disadvantage when no 'give' is wanted. Terylene is not quite so strong as nylon, but is less elastic.

Of the vegetable fibre ropes, hemp, manila, sisal, cotton, and jute (in order of strength) are the most commonly met with. Sisal has become the maid-of-all-work. It is not as smooth or as smart a rope as hemp, manila, or cotton, but it costs less, is very serviceable, and is almost as strong as manila.

Rope, in general, is made by twisting fibres together to form yarn; twisting yarns together to form a strand; then twisting strands together to form a rope. In each process, the twist is made in the opposite direction. The tighter the twist, the harder the rope.

Most ropes have three strands, spiralling from left to right. This is called right-handed hawser-laid rope. Continental hawser-laid ropes are usually left-handed. A rope with four strands twisted right-handed round a central core is called shroud-laid. A large rope made up of three right-handed ropes laid up left-handed is called a cable-laid rope. Hawser-laid ropes are stronger than shroud-laid and cable-laid ropes, in spite of their greater size.

The size of a rope is its circumference, not its diameter. So, as a diameter is about a third of a circumference, a 3-inch rope is about 1 inch thick.

A 3-inch hemp or sisal, hawser-laid rope in good condition will safely take a working load of 10 cwt, allowing for knots (which weaken a rope), friction, and other factors.

The end of a rope you tie a knot with is called the running end, or working end; the rest of the rope is called the standing

Lays of Rope

Hawser-Laid   Left-handed   Shroud-Laid Cable-Laid Braided
Hawser

part. A loop is also called a bight. A bend is a knot which bends (binds, or ties) a rope to another. A hitch is a knot for hitching (fastening) a rope to a fixture such as a post or ring. To 'seize' the end of a rope is to secure it to prevent a knot working loose. To 'mouse' a hook is to close the opening to prevent a rope or eye jumping out.

Some Useful Knots

Sheet Bend: For joining ropes, whether of equal or unequal thickness. When unequal, the thinner entwines the thicker. If there is much difference in thickness, or the ropes are wet or slippery, an extra turn (Double Sheet Bend) makes it more secure.

Reef Knot: Best for tying the ends of the same piece of rope or material, as with bandages and slings and tying parcels. It makes a good first-aid knot because it lies flat against the patient. Tied with one end taken through doubled, the knot becomes a temporary reef (Slip Reef), as used for tying up tent walls or fastening taped tent flaps.

Fisherman's Knot: For joining smooth materials which a sheet bend would not hold, such as thin nylon or gut. Correctly tied, the thumb-knot ends point outwards.

Clove Hitch: For tying a rope to an object such as a post or ring, and for starting and ending most types of lashing. A half-hitch round the standing part prevents the knot untying itself, as it might by the movement of a tethered animal, or a moored boat.

Timber Hitch: For hauling timber. The direction in which the end is twisted back on itself depends on the twist (lay) of the rope. The direction should be with the lay. Because the Timber Hitch is a slip knot, it is used to start a diagonal lashing. Diagonal spars are usually sprung apart, and they are drawn together in a Timber Hitch before being lashed.

Guy-line Hitch: An adjustable knot which can be put into temporary use when a runner breaks.

Stopper Knot: A stop on a rope to prevent it fraying or coming through an eyelet, runner, pulley block, or the like.

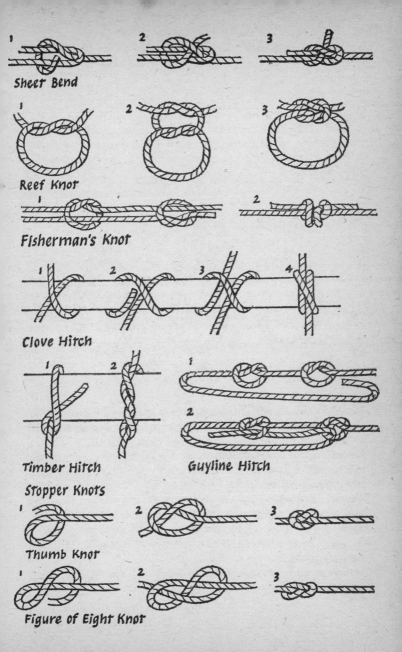

Sheet Bend

Reef Knot

Fisherman's Knot

Clove Hitch

Timber Hitch

Guyline Hitch

Stopper Knots

Thumb Knot

Figure of Eight Knot

Some Rescue Knots

Bowline: The best known of all the loop knots. It can be used for raising or lowering a conscious person, and for water or ice rescue. It is not advisable for dragging an unconscious person because of possible injury to the head and shoulders. A better method is to tie his wrists together with a handkerchief, straddle him on all-fours, with your head through his arms, and move forward with him. The bowline has many uses besides those of rescue.

Bowline

Bowline-on-a-Bight: This is a double loop formed in the middle of the rope, and is used as a sling for an insensible person. He is lowered with one end, and guided clear with the other.

Fireman's Chair Knot: This is also a double loop formed in the middle of the rope, but each loop can be adjusted by a locking half-hitch.

Round Turn and Two Half-hitches: This is one of the best knots for securing a rope to a post, ring, or the like. It is a useful anchor knot (tied to a tree near a cliff edge, for instance) because the round turn takes the strain while the half hitches are being tied.

Double and Triple Sheet Bends: Joining ropes in rescue work, use one of these for safety.

144

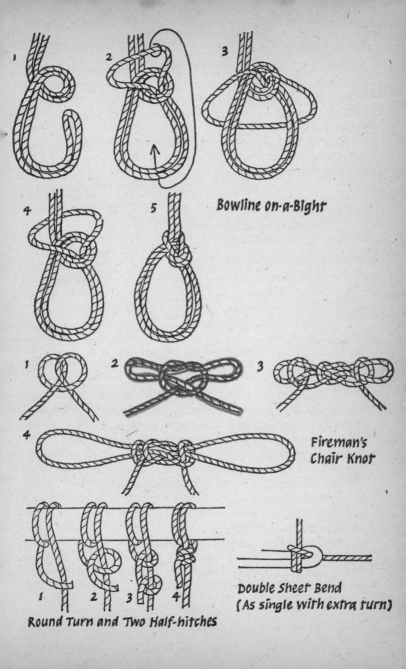

Bowline on-a-Bight

Fireman's Chair Knot

Round Turn and Two Half-hitches

Double Sheet Bend (As single with extra turn)

Whipping

Rope ends should never be allowed to fray. A simple whipping can save a rope which might otherwise become useless.

A rope which cannot be whipped immediately can be temporarily stopped with a thumb-knot, adhesive tape, or short length of twine.

Keep all whipping turns tight from start to finish.

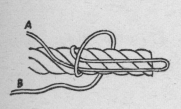

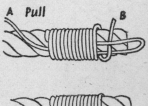

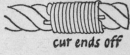

Lashings

There are various ways of lashing (binding) one thing to another with rope or other cordage. In camp and on pioneering projects it is usually sticks, poles, spars, and the like, which are lashed together.

The method of lashing used depends on the position in which the spars are to be lashed together. Spars crossing each other, at any angle and touching, are square-lashed; spars crossing each other but standing apart, thus needing to be drawn together first, are diagonal-lashed; spars to be lashed parallel near their tips, so that they can be opened out to form legs, are sheer-lashed; spars to be lashed parallel without movement, such as the joining of spars to make a flag mast or to bind a broken tent pole, are round-lashed; spars to be lashed to make a tripod are gyn-lashed.

A length of rope used only for lashing is called a lashing.

Square Lashing: This is started with a clove hitch on the more secure of the spars, usually a leg, close to where the other spar crosses. Twist the loose end (about 5 inches long) round the standing part and take it round with the first turn. Make three or four complete turns (as shown), each going inside the previous turn on one side, and outside the previous turn on the other side, so that all turns lie side by side and never override. Next, make two or three frapping (tightening) turns. These go between the spars, across and round the turns already made, drawing them still tighter. Finally, the lashing is finished off with a clove hitch on the spar other than the one started with.

On bridge trestles, the lashings securing the ledger should be started with the clove hitch above it, and those securing the transom should be below it. This is so that the starting clove hitches will be in the best position to take the weight on the transom and the upward thrust on the ledger, should the legs sink into the bed or (with the lock bridge) into the bank. Keep all turns tight.

Diagonal Lashing: This is used mostly where diagonal spars cross and are sprung apart. A timber hitch, running bowline, or other slip knot is tied round the spars at the crossing and they are drawn together. Then about three turns are taken in one direction, and the same in the opposite direction (as shown). Next, two or three frapping turns, then the lashing is finished off with a clove hitch on the most convenient spar.

Sheer Lashing: At the position where the sheer legs are required to open, tie a clove hitch round one spar. Twist the loose end in and make about nine turns round both spars, not too tight to prevent the legs being opened. Next, make one or two frapping turns between the spars, and finish off with a clove hitch on the other spar, and at the other end of the lashing. Sheer legs should not be spread wider than a third of the height of the lashing from the butts.

Round Lashing: This is a straightforward binding lashing. There are no frapping turns. It is started with a clove hitch round both spars, given about nine turns, and finished off with a clove hitch round both spars. On smooth spars the starting clove hitch tends to turn as you pull on the lashing. This is usually remedied by giving the clove hitch an extra inside turn, making it a magnus hitch. Wedges are sometimes used to tighten this lashing.

Gyn Lashing: Also known as the figure-of-eight lashing. A gyn is a tripod normally used for lifting weights with block and tackle. Three spars are laid together with the middle one the opposite way round, as shown. A clove hitch is tied round one of the outer spars, a little way from the tip, and about half a dozen fairly loose turns are woven in and out of the spars. Then two or three loose frapping turns are made between the spars, and the lashing is finished off with a clove hitch on the other outer spar.

Block and Tackle: To lash a block to a spar, tie a clove hitch just above where the block is to be, lay the hook (or eye) of the block against the spar and take about four turns round the hook and the spar, and finish off with a clove hitch round the spar, just below the hook.

Mousing: This is to keep an eye or a rope secure in a hook. The end of a short length of twine is attached by a clove hitch to the back of the hook and several turns are made round the point, then a few frapping turns are made back to the clove hitch and finished off with a reef knot.

Square Lashing

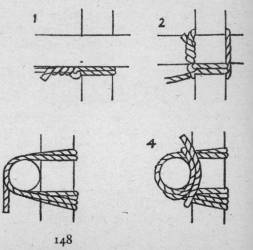

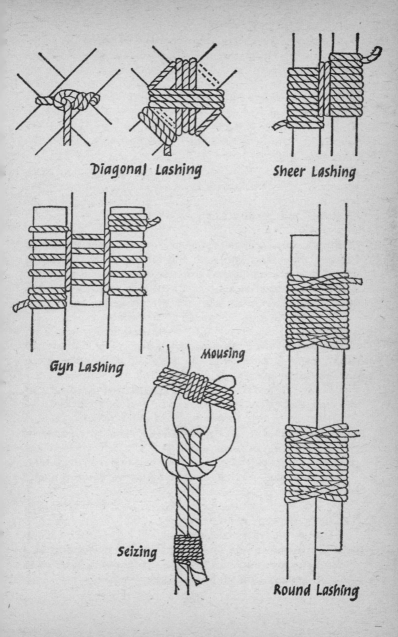

Diagonal Lashing

Sheer Lashing

Gyn Lashing

Mousing

Seizing

Round Lashing

FIRST AID

THE hiker or camper should add to his other skills some knowledge of first aid, so that he will be as capable of dealing with the likely accident as he is of pitching his tent in the dark, lighting a fire in the rain, or of handling any other situation he has trained himself to cope with.

First Aid and Second Aid

In the case of an accident or sudden illness, nature immediately sets to work coping with it. It will form a blood clot over a wound to stop bleeding and keep out destructive germs while it heals the damaged part; and it will knit together a broken bone. But it often needs help – an army of germs might enter before a clot can form; the blood flow might be too strong for a clot to form; the jagged ends of a broken bone might cause further damage owing to careless handling. The kind of help nature needs in cases like these is the aid only a doctor can give – medical aid.

It would be ideal if a doctor and the necessary medical staff and equipment were present at the time of an accident or illness. Instead, owing to distance and other reasons, there is usually an interval of time between the happening of an accident and the receiving of medical aid. It is the help given to the casualty (injured person) in this interval which is so important. It can prevent his condition becoming worse; it can promote his recovery; it can save his life.

If we think of medical aid as second aid, it may help us to realize how dependent its effectiveness can be on good first aid.

Minor injuries do not require medical aid – first aid is the only help nature needs. But inefficient first aid can cause a minor injury to require medical aid later, for example, a simple cut, not properly cleaned, becoming germ infected.

Camp First-aid Kit

This should be kept in a damp-proof box with a close-fitting lid. The contents should be listed, for easy check on necessary replacements, and there should be a note of the nearest doctor's name, address, and telephone number.

Absorbent materials, such as bandages, dressings, and lint, can be kept quite dry in plastic bags closed with elastic bands. Tablets and liquids are best in screw-topped containers, clearly marked. Preparations in tubes last well and are not so readily contaminated by air (and fingers) as in jars or bottles. Cotton wool and lint are best bought in the smallest (sealed) packages you can get. Four 1-oz cartons of lint, for example, can be kept sterile longer than a 4-oz carton, because only 1 oz is open at a time.

Here is a list of contents for a standing-camp first-aid kit. They can be added to, according to necessity, from the village chemist.

Camp First-aid Outfit

DRESSINGS, ETC.
    Sterile dressings – small, medium, large
    Adhesive strip dressings (*Elastoplast type*) – assorted
    Roller bandages – 1-inch, 2-inch, 3-inch
    Crêpe bandages – 4-inch
    Triangular bandages
    Adhesive strapping (*plaster*) – 1-inch roll
    Cotton wool
    Lint, plain (*white*) *and boric* (*pink*)
    Gauze
    Paper tissues

APPLICATIONS, ETC.
    Antiseptic, mild – T.C.P., Dettol, etc.
    Surgical spirit (cleaning instruments; hardening feet)
    Sal Volatile (fainting; bites and stings)

Calamine cream or lotion (sunburn)
Anti-midge preparation
Bicarbonate of Soda (indigestion; bites and stings)
Laxative, mild
Aspirin (headache, pain)

INSTRUMENTS
Scissors, blunt pointed
Tweezers
Safety pins and needles
Medicine glass or measure, graduated
Thermometer, clinical
Small torch

Personal First-aid Kit

For Hike or Expedition

A minimum first-aid kit for a hike or expedition is: sterilized dressings, small and medium – one or two of each (or one 2-inch roller bandage, and cut pieces of lint – 2- and 3-inch squares – two of each, and a small pair of scissors); Elasto-plast-type strips – assorted; and a tube of antiseptic cream suitable for minor burns and cuts. To this can be added aspirin, anti-midge preparation, calamine cream (for sun or wind burn), and a pair of tweezers.

Minor Cuts and Scratches

These and other simple skin injuries require nothing more than well cleaning and a dressing to keep out germs and to protect from further injury. They normally heal in about a week.

In camp, with clean water available, the first-aider starts by washing his hands. Allow wound to bleed a little to help cleanse itself. Clean surrounding area with soap and water and lint (unfluffy side). Do not use cotton wool, because fibres in a wound can delay healing. Clean as close to wound as possible, taking care not to let water or lint touch it, and brushing outwards, away from wound. Put on sterilized dressing. If none available, apply a mild antiseptic to ordinary dressing, or adhesive strip dressing, or to lint (unfluffy side) supported by roller bandage.

Where clean water is not available, apply antiseptic to whatever dressing.

Bleeding can be stopped by applying light pressure on lint pad over wound, or direct thumb pressure if lint, etc., not available, and by raising the part above heart level.

If a wound later becomes inflamed, take the casualty to a doctor.

Bites and Stings

Plant stings and insect bites and stings are generally soon forgotten, and are seldom anything to worry about, unless on the lips or in the mouth. There may be severe pain and swelling, but it is normally short-lived.

Remove any sting, using tweezers or the point of a needle that has been passed through a flame and allowed to cool. Do not use finger and thumb; pressure on the sting's poison bag can drive the poison into the wound. Pain and swelling can be relieved by applying one of the many antihistamine creams, or methylated spirit (keep away from eyes), sal volatile, or bicarbonate of soda (a teaspoonful to a $\frac{1}{2}$-pint mug of water). Plain water gives some ease. If swelling seems excessive, or has not decreased by the next day, take the casualty to a doctor.

For sting in the mouth (usually a wasp taken into mouth on food) give a mouthwash – bicarbonate of soda (in water, as above), or plain water. For sting in throat, give ice to suck or cold water to sip. In both cases take the casualty at once to a doctor.

For animal bite, treat as for a cut. Take the casualty to a doctor, unless the injury is slight.

Fainting

This is due to an insufficient supply of blood to the brain. It may come on suddenly, owing to nerve shock – fright, pain, a horrifying sight, bad news; or gradually, owing to fatigue, long standing, or sitting in a tense or stuffy atmosphere. Recovery is usually fairly rapid under proper treatment.

A person about to faint will appear pale and unsteady. His breathing will be shallow and he will start to sweat. He will feel giddy, cold, and clammy. At this stage, a faint can usually be prevented by pressing his head downwards between his knees if he is already in a sitting position, or by laying him down in a current of fresh air. Loosen tight clothing. Urge deep breathing.

If the person is unconscious, lay him on his back with his head turned to one side, and his feet raised above the level of his head. Loosen any tight clothing about the neck, chest, and waist. Give nothing by the mouth.

When the casualty recovers, give sips of water. If there is no obvious reason for the faint, the casualty should see a doctor.

Burns and Scalds

These are caused by different means – burns by dry heat, scalds by moist heat – but the effects and the treatment are the same. Both are very painful and the quick relief of pain is important.

Minor burns and scalds, where there is only a reddening of the skin or very slight blistering, are treated as for minor skin wounds, by applying a sterile dressing and bandaging firmly.

In the case of severe burns or scalds, the casualty must be got to hospital as soon as possible. Pain can be relieved and the severity of the injury lessened by reducing the temperature of the affected part. The treatment is to immerse the part promptly in cold water, or run cold water over it, for several minutes, then cover lightly. Do not remove adhering clothing, or prick blisters, or apply any lotions or ointments.

Make the casualty as comfortable as possible, and give small and frequent cold drinks.

External Bleeding

Any outward escape of blood from the body (as from a cut) is external bleeding, whether trivial or severe. Internal bleeding (less common) is blood escaping into the body, as when the jagged end of a broken bone damages a blood vessel. A bruise is a form of internal bleeding. Severe loss of blood can mean loss of life.

The object of the first-aid treatment of external bleeding is to keep the blood in, and the germs out. Nature stops bleeding by forming a sealing clot over the escape opening (the wound), but it cannot do it while the blood is still flowing out. So the flowing must be stopped. Water passing along a flexible tube can be stopped by pressing on it against a firm surface, and so it is with a blood vessel pressed against a bone.

Minor bleeding will stop of its own accord, but the pressure of a dressing and bandage, as already explained (see Minor Cuts and Scratches) will stop it sooner.

Severe bleeding must be stopped without delay. Until a dressing (sterilized, if possible, or a pad of any smooth, clean cloth) is available, apply pressure directly over the wound with the fingers, thumbs, or palm. Raise the part (if a limb) above heart level. Place the dressing directly over the wound, press well down, cover with soft padding, and bandage firmly, but

not too tightly. If bleeding continues through the dressing, add further padding and bind a little more tightly. Do not remove the original dressing, it will disturb the clot already forming.

If there is glass (or other foreign body) in the wound, apply pressure round it. Place a dressing lightly over the wound, build a ring or square of pads round it, and bandage firmly.

Blood escapes with less force when sitting, and still less when lying down. Get the casualty to a doctor or hospital.

Shock

Anybody involved in an accident suffers from shock to a greater or lesser degree, depending on the severity of the injury. For the well-being of the casualty, the effects of shock must be lessened as much as possible.

The effects, which are lessened by removing the causes, may be slight enough merely to quicken the breathing rate, or severe enough to bring about complete collapse or worse, if not controlled. Loss of blood and serious burns are two of the most important causes of severe shock.

Good first aid – stopping bleeding, correctly treating injuries, easing of pain, gentle handling, making the casualty as comfortable as possible, reassuring words, and (where necessary) swift removal to hospital – is the best treatment for shock. Shock can be more harmful than the injuries.

Do not move a casualty unnecessarily, or overheat with coverings. Both these can worsen his shocked condition. Never use hot-water bottles: they can cause burns which a casualty may not be able to feel at the time.

The signs and symptoms of shock (signs are what you can see or feel for yourself – swelling, paleness; symptoms are what only the casualty can tell you – pain, giddiness) are similar to those of fainting. Be on the look-out for them.

In minor cases of shock, where the cause does not require hospital treatment, sit or lay the casualty down. A little water, tea, or coffee may be given.

Moving an Injured Person

A casualty's injuries can be made worse by moving him before giving first aid. If for his own comfort or safety he must be moved – danger of falling masonry, moving machinery, fire, electricity or gas, casualty lying across a spar or similar object – the greatest care must be taken, especially if broken bones or fractured spine is suspected.

Fire

If you are the first at the scene of a house fire, at once warn any occupants, and people living on either side. If there is nobody with a private telephone, go or send somebody reliable to the nearest public telephone and report the fire. Give the exact address, and if it is near a well-known public building or landmark, say so. In the country, offer to meet the brigade on the way to guide them to the fire, especially at night.

If it is known that a house on fire is unoccupied, do not open any doors or windows, thus keeping the oxygen content, on which fire depends, at a minimum.

If a fire breaks out in your own home, no attempt should be made to locate it until it is known that everybody is out of the building. A door opened downstairs could let the fire inside rush up the stairs and cut off the means of escape from above.

Searching for anybody, keep as low as possible because there will be more air at ground level. Open all doors carefully. Before turning the handle of a door which opens towards you, put your foot or knee a few inches from it, otherwise fire in the room would blast it open and spread the blaze.

The rescuing of people from burning buildings is best left to professional firemen, except in the gravest emergency, and then only if the rescuer is capable of bringing out a casualty.

A person whose clothes are on fire should be made to lie down to prevent the flames spreading upwards, and then be rolled in a rug or blanket to put them out.

Drowning

A drowning casualty should be given artificial respiration at the earliest possible moment. No time is wasted clearing the mouth or draining out water. Seconds can save life. In water on a sloping bed, the rescuer should start mouth-to-mouth resuscitation as soon as his feet touch the ground, and continue as he wades ashore. Or the rescuer (who may be exhausted) could be met in the water by someone who would immediately take over.

On recovery, the casualty should be seen by a doctor, or sent to hospital.

Electric Shock

In the country, the most likely causes of electric shock casualties are lightning and overhead electric cables. The passage of the current through the body can cause burns at the point of contact and affect nerves, muscles, or heart, and stop breathing.

The treatment of the injuries will vary with each incident. If the casualty is not breathing, artificial respiration is the first and immediate action, then other injuries – severe bleeding first (if any); next, burns. Then to hospital.

Before any treatment can be given, the danger must be removed. No attempt should be made to rescue a person in contact with, or close to, a live high-voltage cable. High voltage can jump a gap. The police must be informed and the cable put out of service. In the meantime, keep at least 20 yards away.

In the case of a person in contact with a low-voltage current, such as the Domestic Supply, immediately break the contact – by switching off; removing the plug; or wrenching the cable free. (No cutting through it with knife or scissors!) If contact cannot be broken, stand on some dry insulating material such as a rubber mat, or folded newspapers, or wood, and push or pull the casualty away.

Always take care that you do not become the next casualty.

Gas Leaks

Gas leak accidents are usually caused by seepage from broken pipes into occupied rooms, and by forgetfulness with slot-meter gas appliances. Car exhaust fumes are just as poisonous. Both are carbon monoxide gas.

Casualties first become confused, pass into a state of stupor, then apparent drunkenness, and finally into a coma.

Before entering a gas-filled room (or garage) take a deep breath and hold it while you fetch the casualty out. If you cannot do so in one breath, turn off the gas (or engine), if possible, and open any windows or doors. If single-handed, fetch the casualty out in stages. Carbon monoxide is lighter than air, so keep low and drag him along the floor. Or he could be dragged out from outside the room (or garage) if there was a rope available. Lying on his back, a loop could be hurriedly placed over his head and shoulders and under his armpits. Work fast. Keep naked lights away.

Apply artificial respiration, if necessary, and get casualty to hospital.

Respiratory Resuscitation

This means artificial respiration. It is a method of getting air into the lungs of a person who has stopped breathing, and who would surely die without the oxygen in the air.

There are several ways of doing this. The latest, and now generally accepted, is the mouth-to-mouth (or to-nose) method. In this method, the first-aider places his mouth over the mouth (or nose) of the casualty and blows air directly into his lungs. The chief advantages of this method over all others are that it is efficient and easy to apply, and can be used where other methods would be impossible, such as standing waist-high in water with a casualty, or down a well. In cases where this method cannot be used (when there are injuries to the face, for example), the approved alternative is the Silvester Method.

The mouth-to-mouth (or to-nose) method requires only that the casualty's head be held in such a position that his tongue

Head right back with neck extended – no obstruction

Tongue can obstruct air passage if casualty is in normal lying position

Mouth-to-Mouth

Mouth-to-Nose

Silvester Method

1 *Remove any obstruction to breathing – head lower than trunk, if possible*

2 *Press casualty's arms firmly over lower chest to force air out of lungs.*

3 *Release pressure by sweeping arms upwards and outwards above his head and backwards as far as possible. Repeat rhythmically about twelve times per minute – 2 seconds, press; 3 seconds, arm lift*

4 *Check mouth frequently for obstruction (mucus, vomit, etc.)*

When natural breathing begins, adjust rhythm to correspond with it.

lies clear of the air passages, instead of falling back and blocking them, as can happen with the normal head position of an unconscious casualty lying on his back.

Prompt action is essential in applying artificial respiration. A casualty who has stopped breathing has only 4 or 5 minutes to live, unless somebody comes to his aid. Watch for chest movement, or listen at nose or mouth to find out if breathing has stopped. Every second counts.

In the mouth-to-mouth method, immediately support the casualty (facing upwards) at the nape of the neck, and press the top of his head backwards, bringing the lower jaw upward and forward. Next, open your mouth wide and take a deep breath, close his nostrils with finger and thumb, seal your lips round his mouth, and blow into his lungs until they are filled. Remove your mouth. Watch the chest subside, then repeat, at the rate of about ten a minute.

Sometimes the mere positioning of the head and the resulting clearing of the airway is enough to start the casualty breathing. When it does, three or four mouth-to-mouth inflations will help.

If the casualty's mouth cannot be sealed, inflate through his nose, sealing his mouth with your thumb. Some consider this to be better and safer than the mouth-to-mouth method.

Practise first, on a training manikin. Never on a person.

Sending for Help

When making an emergency telephone call, give only the bare details. Avoid wrapping them up in a long, rambling story and wasting valuable time. It is best to start off with a general statement, then wait to be asked questions and be ready with the answers.

For example, your camping companion has fallen out of a tree and broken his leg, and from the nearest telephone kiosk you dial 999. The operator answers and you say, 'Ambulance, please. This is Bimble 123' (or whatever exchange and number you are calling from). A voice announces: 'Ambulance Service,' and you say, 'A camper at Oaklea Farm, Bimble, has fallen out of a tree and broken his leg.' Then you wait to be asked any other details required. The person at the other end does nothing but take messages. He knows just what information is required. Finally, give any further information that will be helpful. For instance, the main farm entrance may not be the most suitable approach to the casualty.

Methods of making emergency telephone calls vary, but instructions are usually clearly displayed in call-boxes. When not, dial the operator.

When giving a message, or writing one down for somebody else to telephone or deliver, try to imagine what details you would need if you were the doctor, or the driver of the ambulance, or fire engine, or police car. Names of people and places should be written in block letters.

Do not try to memorize a verbal message word for word. Get the meaning of it in your mind, then reduce it to key words. For example, the message: 'Go and tell them at Oaks Farm that I've run out of oil and I'm stuck on Dibble Hill with the tractor.' could be reduced to: 'Oaks Farm, tractor, Dibble Hill, no oil.'

Homeward tracks

STRIKING CAMP

CAMP is generally struck in roughly the reverse order of pitching, which is the normal way of dismantling anything, but sometimes the weather, meal arrangements, or other reason, makes it advisable to change the order.

A camp may be nothing more than a tent and a fire or stove, but a camp made up of the usual parts – tents, cooking place, wet and dry pits, latrines, and washplace – will normally be struck in that order, though when there are several pairs of hands much of the work is going on at the same time.

The dismantling of non-essentials, such as gadgetry, and jobs such as packing of personal kit and the cleaning of unrequired cooking and other gear, can be done at an earlier stage.

Tents and other canvas should be allowed to dry out thoroughly before packing, especially tent sod cloths, the eaves, and guy-lines.

In wet weather, a tent or awning should be left up, or a groundsheet used for sheltering packed gear and kit.

Striking a tent

Wall-less, one-pole: Slightly slacken main guy. Remove pole and collapse tent gently on to groundsheet. Take out all pegs and tie up guys.

Wall-less ridge: Slacken main guys. Remove back pole, then front pole. Take out all pegs and tie up guys separately.

One-pole, with walls: Take out all side-guy pegs, leaving the wall pegs and main guy to support the tent. Put the pegs aside together – guyless pegs in grass get hidden and left behind. Now, tie up all the side guys. It is much better to do this while the tent is still standing than to grope about for them at ground level among yards of (possibly wet) canvas. Here is a method of tying guys. Extend each guy to its full single length, fold it double (end to end), and repeat the doubling until you have a hank about a foot long. Now, give the hank a slight twist to make a rope of it, and tie the whole into a simple thumb knot. When all the guys are tied, remove the pole, take out all wall and main guy pegs, and tie up main guy.

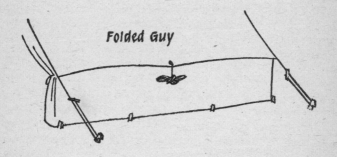

Folded Guy

Ridge with walls: Take out all side-guy and wall pegs, leaving tent supported by main guys. Put pegs aside. Tie up all side guys. Unhook a front and back guy (on same side) and under their control lower the tent away from you. If doing this single-handed, and the second guy cannot be reached without letting go of the first, repeg one of them in a position reachable from the other.

Before packing a tent, all dirt or mud should be scraped or brushed off. Guys should always be tied up to avoid tangling. A sewn-in groundsheet will be damp underneath, and should be wiped dry. Any zips should be unfastened before folding. Pegs, poles, and mallets should be counted, cleaned, and dried. See that they cannot damage tent fabric or groundsheet while packed.

Packing a tent, always roll or fold it towards an open end so that all air is pressed out, so reducing its bulk. If the sod cloth is damp avoid folding it inside the tent. When a tent has to be packed wet, open it out as soon as possible. If you resort to a barn in bad weather do not leave a wet tent packed, certainly not for more than 12 hours. It would be better off standing in the rain.

The Cooking Place

Clean all cooking equipment – the hardware (utensils, kitchen cutlery, etc.) and the software (cloths, muslin, etc.). Wood ash on a wet cloth makes an efficient yet gentle scourer.

Fill in the wet and dry pits when finished with; burn the grease trap off the wet pit, and replace any turf.

Douse the fire when no longer needed and everything burnable has been burned. Better still, let it burn itself out, and so leave less clearing up to do. Soak the place well, and if turf has been removed make sure the ground is not hot when you replace it, otherwise the farmer will later have a withered patch to remember you by. Return any bricks, ironwork, or other cooking aids to where they came from, and put neatly aside any unused or charred wood.

Check before packing that all is complete. It might be wise to do this before filling in the wet and dry pits.

The Rest of the Site

The latrines, and the washplace (unless it is a stream) are normally the last to be dismantled, in that order.

A latrine trench should be filled in to within an inch (or less) of the top, so that the turf (at least 4 inches thick) when replaced will fit into the slight depression and, in nature's own good time, settle down to its normal level. The site of a filled-in latrine is usually marked with a taboo sign made by binding two diagonally crossed sticks to an upright and sticking it in the turf. An easier way is to push two sticks into the turf at opposite angles so that they form a diagonal cross, or to mark a cross in stones. A urinal is returfed at normal level, and not marked.

If the washplace has a sump hole for taking waste water, simply fill in and replace turf, if any.

Taboo Signs

Packing

The order in which personal kit and camp gear are packed when striking camp is the same as originally packed, unless some of it is wet and must be kept away from dry things, or it is necessary to pack dirty cooking gear. The use of plastic bags much simplifies this problem. They are waterproof and add hardly anything in bulk or weight.

The underside of a separate groundsheet is likely to be damp from ground moisture and should be turned over in the open air to dry out. If it has to be packed damp, and is single-faced (cloth one side, rubber or plastic the other) keep the dry and damp sides apart by first folding in half, dry side out. Then fold to required size.

Wet gear packed in a rucksack is little to worry about, if you are likely to be home within a few hours, but it is a very different matter for the hike-camper. Bedding and clothing must be kept dry. If you had to choose between using your groundsheet to protect them from damp things in your rucksack and using it to cover your tent packed on top in the rain, it would be better to let the tent get wet. Of course, if you had a cape which covered both you and your rucksack, the choice would not have to be made.

Before Leaving

Take a final look around the site. Make sure there is no rubbish, no waste food, and not a scrap of litter anywhere.

When you call on the farmer to tell him you are ready to leave, and to pay anything you owe, thank him for allowing you to camp (whether he has charged you for the privilege or not), and ask him if he would like to inspect the site with you. He will probably be too busy, but he will appreciate that to invite inspection is the mark of a good camper, and the kind who is always welcome.

CARE AND STORAGE

THE chief enemy of equipment in storage is dampness. It rots and rusts. The ideal place for storage is a dry room, light, cool, and airy.

When you put your gear away, whether for only a week or for the winter months, it should be in such a condition that it is ready for immediate use.

Tents: Even a rot-proofed tent will rot in time if badly stored. A tent should be thoroughly dry before being put away. Watch double thicknesses at seams and eaves, the bottom edge and sod cloth, and the guys. Brush off any dirt. Wooden pegs are slow to dry and should be packed separately. So should anything which might damage the fabric.

Ideally a tent should be stored hanging opened out over a line or bar. A tent which has to be stored folded during the winter months should be given a periodic airing or two in sun and wind, or at least opened out and fully exposed to the air. Lightly oil metal pole-joints. Use only soap and water for removing dirty marks. Detergents affect the proofing.

The off-season, October to February, is the best time to do repairs and make replacements. It is also the time when the firms who undertake repairs and reproofing can give their promptest service.

All canvas and leather goods, not forgetting rucksacks, should be treated in the same way as tents to prevent mildew attack. Mildew has a musty smell, and is seen as greyish spots or patches which cannot be entirely removed. An affected part should be carefully brushed and exposed to sun and air. Reproofing of the area is likely to be necessary.

Groundsheets: The plastic groundsheet, now ousting the rubberized type, is unaffected by mildew, oil, or grease, and requires little attention other than being stored clean and dry. Adhesive tape will repair holes or tears.

Rubberized groundsheets should be kept free from oil and grease – they perish rubber. Any soiled part should be wiped clean at once. Holes and tears can be repaired either with rubber patch and solution on the rubber side, or adhesive tape on the fabric side. Store completely dry, particularly the fabric side. French chalk dusted on the rubber side will keep it more supple. It also prevents the rubber on ageing groundsheets from sticking. Wipe off before use.

Sleeping Bags: These require little attention. They should be stored folded loosely. First-aid sticking plaster will temporarily repair a tear and save loss of down or feather filling. Sleeping bags with synthetic fillings, such as Terylene, Dacron, and Tricel can be washed at home. It should be done by hand (no twisting or rubbing) in lukewarm water and mild soap-flakes, then thoroughly rinsed in lukewarm water and hung up to drip dry. Bags with down, feather, kapok, felt, flock, and similar fillings can only be cleaned satisfactorily by dry cleaning, and should always be thoroughly aired before use. The fumes can be fatal.

Kitchenware: Dixies and similar hardware should be stored clean and dry. Anything rustable should be rubbed over with vaseline on a clean cloth, and washed out with hot water before use. Mops, scrubbers, cloths, and muslin should be washed out and dried.

Pressure Stoves: Replace washers no longer sealing perfectly. Renew jet if worn (always use correct size of pricker). Seeping at the filler cap when under pressure means a damaged seal and a loss of pressure. Replace filler cap. Always use correct size of spanner. Pliers and misfit spanners damage nuts. Store stove drained, cleaned, and dried.

Axes and Saws: Rub linseed oil well into axe handles, and wipe lightly. Grease axe heads with vaseline or other grease, not forgetting the cutting edge, and cover with its own mask or sacking. If storage conditions are too dry, and the natural moisture content of an axe handle is reduced, the head will become loose. Remedy by standing it in water for a few hours. Bow saws should be stored with the blade left in and, like other saws, should be cleaned, greased, and masked with a strip wrapping or other suitable means.

Ropes and Spars: Rope, like canvas, should be dried (by hanging loosely under cover) before storing. It is best stored hung in coils. Right-handed ropes (hawser laid) should be coiled right-handed (clockwise), and left-handed ropes, anti-clockwise. All rope ends should be whipped or spliced to prevent unravelling.

Spars and long tent poles should not be placed in a way that allows them to sag in the middle, such as leaning against a wall, or lying flat supported only at each end. The sag will set itself in the timber. Spars are best stored lying flat, off the ground, and supported at sufficient intervals to prevent sagging, and spaced to give each a good circulation of air. Out of doors with only a roof covering makes good storage.

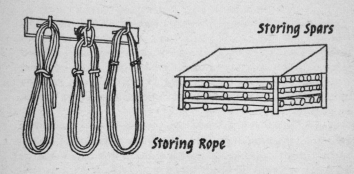

Storing Spars

Storing Rope

Appendices

Keeping Logs

A log is a kind of diary. It is a record of something happening over a period of time, such as a journey, a record of the weather, or bird or animal observation. This meaning of the word comes from the old sailing-ship days when a ship's speed was ascertained by letting out a log on a knotted line from the stern and timing with an hour-glass the number of knots which passed over the stern in a given time. The number of knots was then recorded in the ship's log book, along with date, time, position, and other details.

A log, like a diary, is a bit of history. Some history books make dreary reading. Let yours be interesting reading.

Hike or Expedition Logs

A log written as part of a test, such as the Advanced Scout Standard hike and Duke of Edinburgh Award expedition, is usually called a report. That is because an account of it has to be seen by (reported to) an examiner. It is still a log, but while writing it keep in mind the stranger (examiner) who will later be reading it. Try to make him feel, having read it, that he has actually been with you on the journey.

Include everything asked for by the examiner. It should be possible for a stranger to make the journey without any help but the log. A page (or double page) showing a sketch map of the whole route (copied from a map and, if necessary, enlarged) makes a log more useful as well as more interesting.

The log itself is not written on the journey, only the rough notes. Jot these in a pocket notebook not too small for making sketches. Note times, distances (checked by map), weather, and general description of route ('crossed plank bridge and took footpath through barley field to little church with red-topped tower'). Small route sketches are useful where the way is difficult to explain. Let your log show your knowledge of the countryside and wild life, but if you are a specialist in anything (butterflies, fungi, for example) don't hog the log with it.

Write out the log itself as soon after the event as possible, while everything is fresh in your mind. Take care over it, and make as good a job of it as you can. Quarto (10 inches by 8 inches) is a good size. Log books can be bought with blank pages for sketches or photographs.

There are usually no rules about the lay-out of the log, but one popular form has its pages ruled with one narrow column on the left showing times, and two on the right giving point-to-point distances and progressive mileage. Use block capitals for each place-name and add its map reference, if necessary.

You will produce a better log if you first do a short practice one or two.

Specimen Log

	EXPEDITION LOG		
TIME	SATURDAY · JULY 9th	MILES	
2·15	Sky overcast. Wind moderate, S.W. Set off from NEW BIGTON railway station (MR 312317) taking the LINGLY road SE towards POPTON.	0	0
2·30	Left main road and crossed stile at foot path to BOGGLE	¾	
2·45	(SW). at NAB FARM	½	1¼

BIGTON   N

LINGLY

NAB FARM

1 inch to 1 mile

Patrol Log Books

Little can be said about maintaining a Patrol log book already in full swing, because it is simply a matter of continuing as before. However, if you are the new Scribe taking over for two months, keep the log alive and going at least as well as it was before you took over. Keep it up to date. Enter it up as soon as possible after each meeting or event. A log that is left for weeks unentered is usually a lifeless thing and reads like an almanac.

If your Patrol has no log book, now is a good time to begin one. A Patrol with a live log is a Patrol with roots, and its log becomes its most treasured possession.

To make a start, you cannot do better than read *Keeping Log Books* No. 10 in The Patrol Books series.

Keeping a Nature Diary

Keeping a nature diary about birds and animals means observing them every day, if possible, and writing down what you have observed.

Use a notebook as big as will go into your pocket. Give it its title – NATURE DIARY – on the outside cover. On the inside cover, or on the first page, write your name, Patrol and Troop, and the dates covering the period of observation. State also the place of observation, if all the observations are to be made at one place. If they are not, state the place as you make each entry. In either case, a rough sketch map on the inside cover or the centre pages, showing the place, or places, of observation, will be helpful to the examiner.

Do not divide your diary up into days beforehand, because you may sometimes need more space than you have allowed yourself. Start each day at the top of a new page, giving place of observation (if necessary), time, day, date, and briefly stating the prevailing weather conditions. Keep all your notes short, and give each observation a separate paragraph. Sketches (of tracks, etc.) make a nature diary more interesting.

If, as is probable, your diary is likely to look the worse for wear by the end of the observation period, make your notes separately and rewrite them later.

Bird and animal distribution varies from place to place, and obviously the range is smaller in the town than in the country. Birds, being more numerous and in greater variety than animals, are in general easier to observe than animals. In the town they can be observed in public parks and gardens, and in private gardens a cat-proof bird table or nesting box can attract enough bird activity for any observer, whether simply identifying and recording the different kinds, or concentrating on the behaviour and habits of one species, or even of one particular bird.

Some animals, such as squirrels and hedgehogs, are not uncommon in town green spots, but it is in the fields and woods where most of our wild animals have their natural haunts. Many are night hunters and are fairly inactive during the day. The animal watcher keeps his eyes wide open. He learns to move quietly, to hear without being heard, to sit or stand patiently still where he can see without being seen and where the wind is not carrying his scent towards the animal. To watch fox or badger cubs at play is reward enough for any amount of time spent patiently watching and waiting.

Always remember never to interfere with the normal life of a wild creature. Do nothing that may cause it to seek a new home or to desert its young. And get permission before entering private property.

Collection of Leaves and Flowers

The best time of year for collecting leaves and flowers is late spring to early summer. May is the best month for flowers, but there is hardly a time of year when there is none to be found.

The specimens you gather cannot really be called a collection until they are mounted and identified.

Select your flower specimen before you actually gather it, rather than pick it and throw it away because of some blemish.

When collecting tree leaves remember the difference between a leaf and a leaflet. Compound leaves, such as ash, elder, horse chestnut, and laburnum, are made up of pairs of leaflets and a terminal (top) leaflet. The whole set is the leaf. Select leaves of average size. Leaves near the foot of a tree are usually

bigger than average.

Flowers are best mounted on loose-leaf sheets of fairly firm quality and held in position with Sellotape. Before mounting, they must be kept under pressure for a few days to dry out. Do this by arranging one or more flowers on four or five thicknesses of blotting paper or newspaper cut to the size of the loose leaf sheet or whatever they will finally be mounted on, then place an equal thickness of paper on top and arrange the next flower(s) on top of that, and repeat the process. With the last protective thickness on the top, either place the lot under heavy books or bind them between hard covers.

Leaves can be treated in the same way, but between fewer thicknesses, or between the pages of a book.

After mounting, enter the name of each specimen and, in the case of flowers or uncommon trees, when and where it was found.

Weather Log

A simple weather log can be kept without using meteorological instruments, but readings from a thermometer and a barometer make the job more useful and more interesting.

The observations that can be recorded without instruments are: weather (rain, fine, etc.); sky (cloud amount); wind (direction); remarks (blustery, muggy, etc.). To these can be added temperature and barometric pressure. If the observer can identify clouds, and has a copy of the Beaufort Scale (for estimating wind force by observation), and a rain gauge, he can add columns for cloud types, wind force, and rainfall.

With or without instruments, a weather log is of little value unless the recordings are made at the same time (preferably twice) each day. The observer should choose times which make this possible. Morning and evening are good times, and noon if possible.

Use the Beaufort letters in your Weather and Sky columns: r = rain; d = drizzle; s = snow; rs = sleet (rain-snow); h = hail; p = shower (p = passing, pr = rain shower, ps = snow shower, etc); t = thunder; l = lightning; w = dew; z = haze; m = mist; f = fog; F = thick fog. A small letter doubled means 'continuous'; a capital letter means 'heavy'; a double capital letter means 'heavy continuous'. For example, dd = continuous drizzle; R = heavy rain; SS = continuous heavy snow.

The Beaufort sky letters are: b (blue) = sky less than $\frac{1}{4}$ covered by cloud; bc (blue-cloud) = about half covered by cloud; c (cloudy) = $\frac{3}{4}$ or more covered by cloud; o (overcast) = completely covered by cloud.

Weather logs make fascinating study. Note how change of wind direction and other variations forewarn certain types of weather.

Clouds

There is always a certain amount of water vapour in the air. Being a gas, water vapour is invisible, but when it is cooled it condenses (thickens) into visible water droplets, so light that they remain airborne. A cloud can be described as a mass of water vapour condensed into visible water droplets by cooling. If the cooling continues, the water droplets increase in size as they further condense and, becoming too heavy to remain airborne, they fall as rain. Snow and ice (hail) are the result of even further cooling and condensation. Mist or fog is cloud that has formed at ground level.

The molecules of which water is composed behave as if they have no liking for heat or cold. When water is heated in a pan, the molecules begin escaping from the surface in their millions, and so continue until they have all gone and the pan is dry. But they have not gone far before they find themselves where it is too cold for them and they seemingly huddle together (condense) into visible water droplets, appearing as a cloud of steam. Cold wall tiles or pipes in the room would further cool and condense any steam that touched them, turning it back into water. If the air in the room was dry enough it would gradually soak up the cloud of droplets, which would become invisible water vapour and might eventually find themselves miles high as part of a cloud in the sky.

Condensation can take place in any part of the atmosphere where sufficient water vapour exists. The greatest height at which clouds of any substance form is about 40,000 feet, or about $7\frac{1}{2}$ miles.

In general, clouds take the shape either of lumpy masses or level sheets, or of a combination of the two. The lumpy types are called 'cumulus' – Latin for a 'heap', and the sheet types are called 'stratus', meaning a 'sheet'. There is also a type which has a feathery, fibrous appearance, called 'cirrus' – Latin for a 'curl' or a 'lock of hair'.

Clouds, then, are named according to their appearance. There are ten main types, and they are divided into three groups – high (above 20,000 feet), medium (6,500 to 20,000 feet), low (under 6,500 feet). Two of the types are not included in any of these groups because their development is vertical rather than horizontal and a single cloud can extend through all three levels, having its base at 3,000 feet and its top at 25,000 feet, or more.

Most cloud forms are associated with a particular kind of weather. The atmospheric pressure system known as a 'low' or 'depression', brings us most of our wet weather. It usually comes from the south-west and has a regular cloud sequence, which is a useful guide to the approach of depression weather.

Here are brief descriptions of the ten cloud forms and the weather associated with them. The letters in brackets are the abbreviations used by meteorologists internationally.

Cirrus (Ci): This high cloud, like the other two cirrus types, is composed of ice crystals instead of water droplets. That is why all cirrus clouds have a whitish appearance. They are also without shadow. Cirrus is a whispy, fibrous detached cloud and takes many forms, often resembling tufts, feathers, 'mares' tails', and the like. They are seen in fine weather, but coming from the south-west they are usually the first sign of an approaching depression, though it will be hours, or even days, away.

Cirrocumulus (Cc): Small rounded masses, often resembling rippled sand, or a pebbly beach, a flock of sheep. The herringbone form it sometimes takes is popularly known as 'mackerel sky'. They usually indicate a change from fine weather to unsettled rainy weather of short duration.

Cirrostratus (Cs): A whitish veil of cloud. This is the next cloud in the depression sequence. It is the cloud which gives the sun or moon its halo. No other cloud does, so a halo means cirrostratus, and indicates approaching rain if the halo gradually disappears and the sky remains overcast.

Altocumulus (Ac): This and the next one are the medium height clouds, although 'alto' means 'high'. It is similar in appearance to cirrocumulus but on a bigger scale, thicker, less white, and has shadow. This cloud, unlike any other, sometimes produces an inside-out halo, called a corona, its outside edge being red-rimmed. A halo's inner rim is red. It is a sign of rain when a corona is seen to grow smaller (due to increasing size of cloud droplets), and a good sign if it grows larger. Otherwise, this cloud has little weather significance.

Altostratus(As): A greyish veil of cloud through which the sun or moon is seen as a watery disc. It is the next in the depression sequence. If wet weather is approaching, the watery disc will disappear and the cloud will thicken and darken. It may even begin to rain.

Stratocumulus (Sc): A low, lumpy or rolling mass of dull grey cloud, usually covering most of the sky, but often thin enough in parts for the blue to be seen through. It is not a weather indicator, and rarely produces rain.

Cirrus

Cirrocumulus

Cirrostratus

Altocumulus

Altostratus

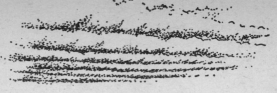

Stratocumulus

Stratus

Nimbostratus

Cumulus

Cumulonimbus

Stratus (St): A uniform layer of cloud like fog off the ground. It is the lowest of the clouds, often lower than 500 feet, and on high ground is described as hill fog. It is not a rain cloud, but can produce drizzle if carried uphill on the wind.

Nimbostratus (Ns): 'Nimbus' means a 'rain cloud', and that is what it is. It is the last in the depression cloud sequence and can give hours of rain. It is a low and gloomy, ragged, watery-looking cloud, and what it usually tells you about the weather is that it is already raining.

Cumulus (Cu): This is the easiest to identify. It is the cauliflower-topped cloud like a heap of cotton wool with a flat base. There are two types. The white soft-looking ones drifting slowly across the sky are called 'fair-weather' cumulus and promise fine, calm weather. The other type is the 'shower' cumulus. It is a much bigger cloud, developing to a great height from a long base line and sending up many rounded heads. This cloud gives the sudden heavy showers.

Cumulonimbus (Cb): The thunder cloud. It is similar to shower cumulus, but is darker and angrier-looking, and develops mountainous towers reaching about 20,000 feet high which sometimes flatten out at the top to form an anvil shape. This is the cloud which gives us hail, the thunder shower, and lightning, as well as strong gusty wind.

Safety Precautions

Before you set out on any adventurous pursuit or activity, do not risk having it ruined by neglecting necessary precautions.
Hill Walking: Always take your map and compass, no matter what the weather at the time, or how well you know the route. Take a windproof anorak, warm underclothing and outerclothing, breeches or long trousers, broken-in walking boots with two or three pairs of socks, and spare clothing including woollen headgear and gloves.

Have a good meal before you start, and take emergency rations (chocolate, barley sugar, dried fruit, etc.). Carry a small first-aid kit, a whistle, and a torch. Leave word where you are going, and keep to your route. Travel in a party of four or more. Know where the nearest telephone is, and whether there is a local Mountain Rescue Post. The mountain distress signal is six blasts on the whistle, repeated at minute intervals.

Sailing: Do not sail a boat, canoe, or punt unless you are competent to handle it, and be sure it is seaworthy. Be able to swim. Changing places in a small boat, crouch low, one at a time, and keep to the centre line, holding the sides. Never attempt to change places in a canoe. In the event of a capsize, stay with the craft unless it is drifting into danger. Rescuers will see a boat more easily than a bobbing head.

With bigger craft, boat equipment, distress signalling, fire-fighting and life-saving equipment should all be checked before setting sail. All crew on a sailing craft should wear life-jackets. Get the latest weather and tidal information. Do not overload the boat. Whenever afloat avoid wearing rubber boots and other heavy clothing. Life-belts should be thrown near the person in distress, not at him.

Other Pursuits: Before venturing into any new activity that has an element of danger in it, seek the advice of the experts, and take it. Never underrate sensible precautions, or over-estimate your own ability, and you will come to little harm.

SCOUT BADGE REQUIREMENTS
(*the numbers in brackets refers to pages in this book*)

The Scout Standard

ONE: LOOKING AFTER YOURSELF

(*a*) Pack a rucksack (17) for a weekend camp (11)
(*b*) Prepare a personal first-aid kit for an expedition (152)
(*c*) Light a fire (103) make a hot drink (120) cook a simple meal out of doors (118)
(*d*) Pitch (84) and strike (164) a hike tent
(*e*) Camp out for at least one night; or, in winter spend at

least one night in a hostel or hut as part of a Scout activity

TWO: HELPING OTHER PEOPLE
  (a) Know how to deal with cuts (152) stings (153) burns (154) and fainting (154)
  (b) Show ability to direct strangers and have some knowledge of local public transport services and local places of interest or importance, including the location of doctors, police station, fire alarms, and public call-boxes

THREE: GETTING ABOUT
  (a) Set a map (65) know what is meant by a compass bearing (51)
  (b) Show understanding of scale (60) and conventional signs (63) by describing a short route selected on an Ordnance Survey map
  (c) Go on a 10 kilometre (6-mile) hike with a friend of your own age, and on return make a verbal report of a set objective achieved *en route* (e.g. sketch or obtain specific knowledge about some place or person). This may be carried out at home or abroad
  (d) Demonstrate an understanding of the Country and Highway Codes (43)
  (e) Find out about a foreign country, work out an interesting route to it, and tell your Patrol about the main things you would expect to find there

FOUR: SCOUTING SKILLS
  (a) Explain how to use and care for a knife (130) and axe (131). Use a knife to whittle a tent peg (or other object) from a piece of wood (139) and an axe to prepare wood for a fire (138)
  (b) Demonstrate any three knots, bends or hitches and two lashings useful in camp or in a boat (142)
  (c) Show a general knowledge and interest in weather conditions and signs and, where appropriate, relate these to your home area
  (d) Know the Country Code (43)

Demonstrate to your Patrol or Troop some skill or proficiency in a personal hobby or interest. Examples: cycling, swimming, nature study, weather lore, aircraft recognition, stars, horse-riding, model-making, basket work, stamp collecting, literature, drawing, radio construction, decorating, joinery.

These are examples only, and other interests or pursuits may qualify.

The Advanced Scout Standard

ONE: SELF RELIANCE
(a) Have camped twelve nights
(b) Swim 45 metres (50 yards) (Alternatives only permissible at the discretion of the District Commissioner)
(c) Understand the precautions that must be taken, including a knowledge of hypothermia (exposure) (187), its causes, prevention, symptoms and immediate treatment before setting out on an adventurous activity, e.g. sailing, hill walking and caving (181)
(d) Complete any two of the following:
   i Be able to operate (107) and maintain a pressure stove (169)
   ii Know what to look for when choosing a camp site (81) and draw up a complete menu (including quantities) for a two-man weekend camp (111)
   iii Cook a two-course meal for two people in a kitchen or galley (120)

TWO: SERVICE
(a) Show how to give clear, concise information when calling for an Ambulance, the Police, or Fire Brigade, (162) and know what action to take in the event of an accident

or other emergency, including rescue from fire (157) drowning (158) electric shock (158) and gas leak (159)

(b) Know the first-aid treatment for external bleeding (155) and shock (156) the correct method of applying respiratory resuscitation (159) and the dangers involved in moving injured persons (157)

(c) Carry out some form of voluntary service within or outside Scouting, either by doing a worthwhile job of at least 3 hours' duration, or by performing regular service for an equivalent period. This may be carried out at home or while on a visit abroad

THREE: ADVENTURE

(a) Complete either a 20-kilometre (12-mile) journey on foot or by water or a 80-kilometre (50-mile) cycle journey, camping out overnight with a Scout of your own age. Produce a brief written account of your journey and of what has interested you. This may be carried out in the United Kingdom or as part of a visit abroad

(b) Use a prismatic or Silva-type compass outdoors to complete a simple exercise involving compass bearings (48)

(c) Explain the contour system (62) and be able to give and locate an Ordnance Survey grid reference (69)

(d) Complete any two of the following:

    i Take part with your own Patrol or Troop in a joint outdoor activity with a Patrol from another Troop, either from the United Kingdom or abroad, e.g. camp, hike, wide game, or expedition

    ii Go alone or with a friend of your own age: either to a place of interest or on a journey of not less than 40 kilometres (25 miles) using public transport. Give a brief verbal report on the day's events

    iii Either paddle a single-seat canoe for 1500 metres (1 mile) or crew a sailing dinghy round a triangular course or understand the delay system and abseil properly down 9 metres (30 feet)

    iv While camping abroad spend a day with your Patrol or another Scout from your own or a local Troop in exploring a local town or village. On your return, report verbally on what you did, what you saw, whom you met, and what you learnt of local life.

(a) Complete a pioneering project using at least two different lashings and/or blocks and tackle (146) (This should normally be a Patrol project)

(b) Demonstrate three knots, bends or hitches useful in rescue (144)

(c) Either cook a backwoods meal and eat it (126) or make a bivouac and sleep in it (87)

(d) Know the safety rules of axemanship (134) and how to care for a bush saw (170) and felling axe (170). Use either for felling, trimming, or logging up light timber (136)

(e) Complete any two of the following:

 i Either keep a nature diary about birds and animals over a period of at least one month (173) or make a specimen collection of leaves and flowers over a similar period (174)

 ii Either keep a simple daily weather record for one month (175) or maintain the Patrol log for two months (173)

 iii Either visit an important building or other local feature and compile a short report about it, describing its history and purpose; or survey a small area in the vicinity of your home, e.g. half mile of river or canal and construct a large-scale plan showing its important features

 iv Show attainment of a skill or interest by passing a Pursuit badge

 v Demonstrate an awareness of the need for conservation by actively taking part in a conservation project

(f) Discuss with your Scout Leader:

 i Your understanding of the Scout Promise and Law

 ii Your future Scout training and membership of the Venture Scout Section

 iii The practical meaning of the worldwide brotherhood of Scouts

Hypothermia

What it is: Hypothermia is the medical term for excessive cooling of the body. It is a serious condition, and can be fatal. Out of doors, it usually results from exposure to bad weather conditions in which the casualty is in a wet-cold state, combined with other factors such as fatigue, anxiety, and hunger. It can happen on the hills, in camp, afloat, on the sportsfield, to the elderly and infirm at home, or in any other wet-cold exposure situation.

Cause: The commonest cause is wet-cold exposure accompanied by exhaustion. A typical casualty is the inadequately equipped hiker, wet through in a cold wind and physically exhausted; his temperature, which he is unable to maintain owing to exhaustion, falls drastically and unless the heat loss is arrested his body becomes chilled to the core, and this adversely affects the functions of the vital organs (particularly the heart and brain), and collapse and death follow.

Signs and symptoms: These are easily overlooked in the early stages. They can progress from a mere sluggishness and complaints of coldness and tiredness to total collapse, all within a period of an hour or two. Early signs, one or more of which may appear, and in no fixed order, are: slowness of physical and mental response; abnormal behaviour, sometimes reckless; clumsiness and stumbling; speech slurred, and vision and hearing sometimes affected; sudden shivering fits, and cramps. If the condition continues to deteriorate, collapse, stupor and loss of consciousness will follow, ending in death.

Treatment: In all situations of wet-cold exposure the treatment must at once be aimed at preventing further loss of body heat, and at raising the inner (core) temperature. Ideally, the casualty should immediately be got into dry clothing, wrapped up warm and insulated against further heat loss, and (if conscious) given hot drinks. Casualties dealt with effectively in the early stages normally revive without any special treatment, but in the more advanced stages medical attention is essential and needed urgently.

The serious cases of exposure and exhaustion that occur in

parties of walkers and climbers are frequently due to in-experienced leadership, often in the mistaken belief that to stop or turn back is a sign of weakness; and in being unaware of the possible deadly consequences of pressing on when all is not well with the party.

AT THE FIRST SIGNS OF DISTRESS IN HIS PARTY, THE EXPERIENCED LEADER CALLS A HALT, UNLESS HE KNOWS THAT THERE IS SHELTER ONLY MINUTES AWAY. HE DOES NOT PRESS ON AND RISK THE ONSET OF EXHAUSTION AND A POSSIBLE FATAL CASE OF HYPOTHERMIA. His aim will be: to provide for the casualty whatever weatherproof shelter he can (natural, tent, waterproof sheeting, mountaineer's man-sized polythene bag, etc.); to get him dried and warm (in spare clothing), and insulated against cold, with extra padding underneath (in sleeping bag or blankets, in spare clothing, or in mountaineer's man-sized polythene bag drawn in at the neck and with the head protected in a muffler, etc., or huddled between fit members); if possible, to give hot drinks (condensed milk, etc.) and/or nourishment (glucose tablets, chocolate, raisins, Kendal mint cake, etc.); and to get help, if needed.

NEVER try to externally heat an exposure casualty, either by rubbing, using hot water bottles, or by any other such means. This will cause further deterioration and can kill, because warm blood is then drawn from the vital organs to the cold body surface, where it is cooled and returns to lower the core temperature even further. Alcoholic drinks, such as brandy, are equally dangerous. Keep any plastic weather protection away from the casualty's face, because static electricity causes plastic to cling to the skin, and suffocation can result.

A stretcher case has a better chance of survival if he is made dry and warm and well insulated all round against cold before being transported, and also if carried with the head kept slightly lower than the feet. Carried wet and cold may save time, but it can lose a life. On arrival at base or other suitable shelter, the best treatment is rapid rewarming in a bath as hot as a fit person can comfortably bear, preferably supervised by a doctor.